Aspects of Art

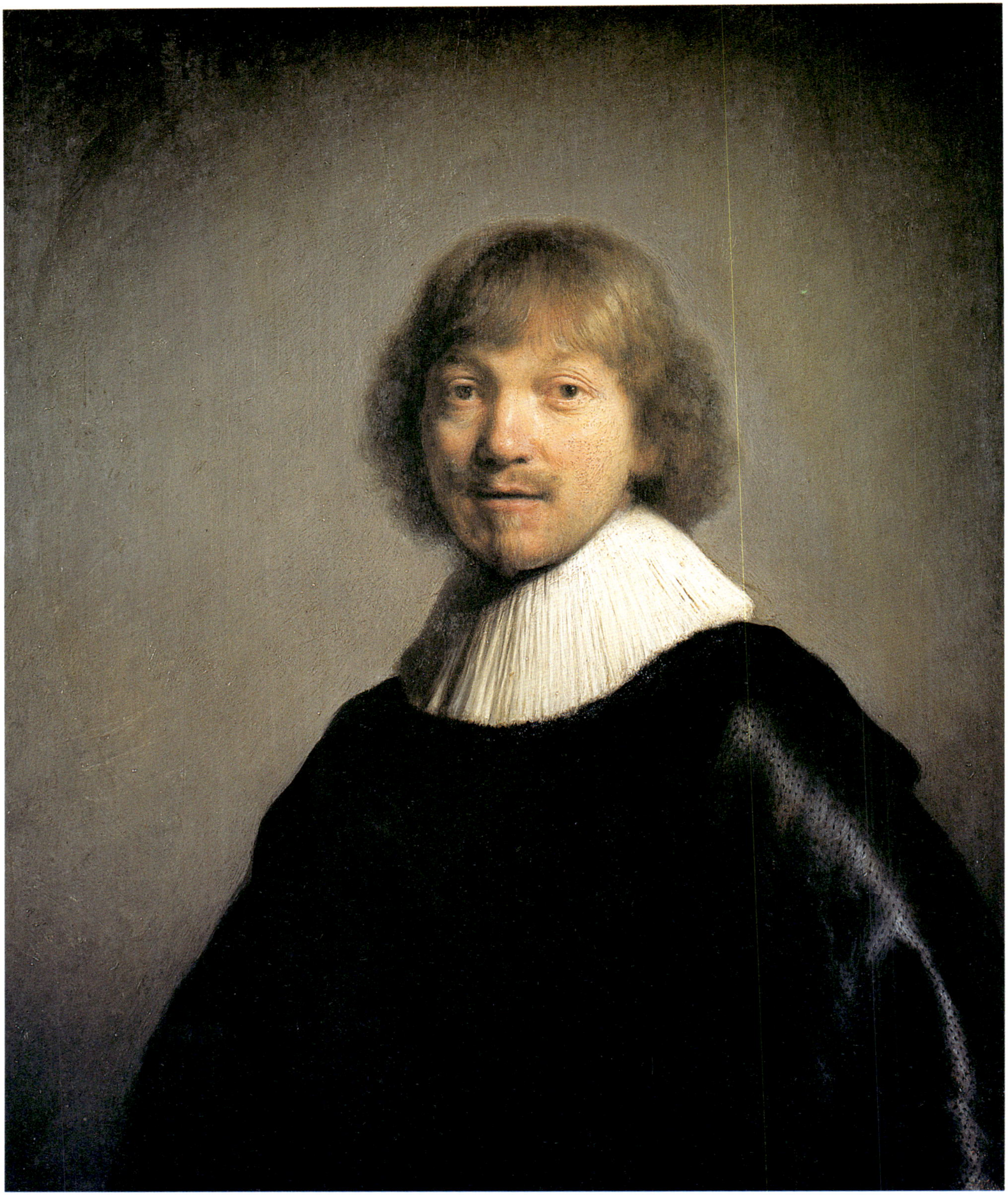

Aspects of Art

A Painter's Alphabet

based on the collection at Dulwich Picture Gallery

Tom Phillips

Bellew Publishing London

First published in Great Britain in 1997
by Bellew Publishing Company Limited

Bellew Publishing Company limited
8 Balham Hill, London SW12 9EA

Designed by Ray Carpenter

Production by
Supreme Publishing Services
Printed in Italy by Vallardi
Typesetting: Banbury Pre-Press

ISBN 1 85725 111 3

Contents

for Arabella & Flora

Preface

Paintings are often read as documents and galleries visited as archives. Of course images from the past tell us an astonishing amount about the society which produced them, but that is not what they were made to do. Art is a response to the visual world; it is an enthralling communication of stories, ideas, loves and hates. This response and this communication can be as vital now as when the paint was still wet. Old master paintings help us to see, understand and enjoy the world around us.

Dulwich Picture Gallery houses an unrivalled collection of masterpieces from the seventeenth and eighteenth centuries. Our education department has shown that none of these works have lost their power to delight, to move and to communicate with children and adults from every background and culture. A most generous grant from the Leopold Muller Estate has enabled this mission to be pursued through a series of publications, available to a wider audience than could ever take advantage of the Gallery's Education programmes themselves. From the first it was decided that one of the series should be written by a practising artist, who would instinctively regard paintings as incomplete experiments in looking.

In Tom Phillips the Gallery has found the ideal creative commentator: an artist of bewildering range and imagination, and a writer of elegance and insight. His text is full of surprises; or as he puts it 'chance and risk are at the heart of the artistic enterprise'. He opens up the experience of art, exploring the overlap between creating and responding. The clarity of the writing masks the complexity of the issues. Tom Phillips's questioning leads in a daunting variety of directions, but this is an essential journey of discovery for those who believe in life beyond the label.

Desmond Shawe - Taylor *(Director)*

A is for Abstract

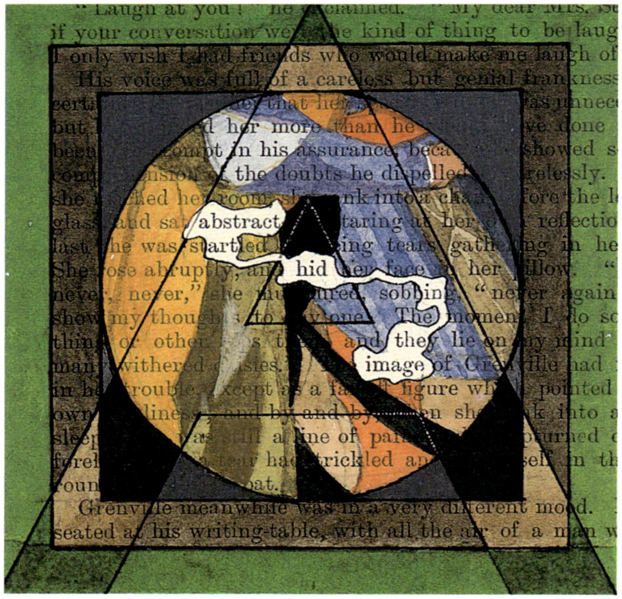

Abstract art refers to nothing outside itself. This would make it seem easy: anything goes. In fact it is hard to do successfully because we are from birth constantly striving to work out what we see; to interpret visual data as real things in the world. From this comes the unbidden habit of seeing animal shapes in clouds and imagining that the blotches of the moon's surface are a smiling head. Recent research even suggests that we have a special and refined program in our brains solely reserved for reading faces. To roam freely in a region of pure colour and configuration is a triumph against these tendencies in the artist and his audience: perhaps this is why abstraction (outside the world of ornament and decoration) (p.40) appears so late in the history of art.[1]

To put this the other way around, however, every picture is an abstract before it is anything else. The organisation of its surface, the balance of light and dark, the disposition of colours, the tension of outlines, all belong to the abstract qualities of the painting. It can interest us or displease us before we know what it is about.

If there is life and art on the planet of some other sun and its inhabitants by some warp of chance have received this book, they (who know nothing of noses or clothes or rivers and roofs) would have to judge our pictures on their abstract virtues alone: as we would theirs. My guess is that their preferences, unencumbered by association, might well be the same.

As well as being an aspect of entire pictures abstract forms inhabit the interior of every painting. The initial letter 'A' here includes a fragment of Poussin's *Triumph of David* (p.25). The dreamlike excerpt on this page comes from the edge of another Poussin (p.63) and shows the great and usually meticulous artist improvising at speed and handling areas of warm and cool colours with only the vaguest landscapy references (plus half a wing) which disappear when we remove the context.

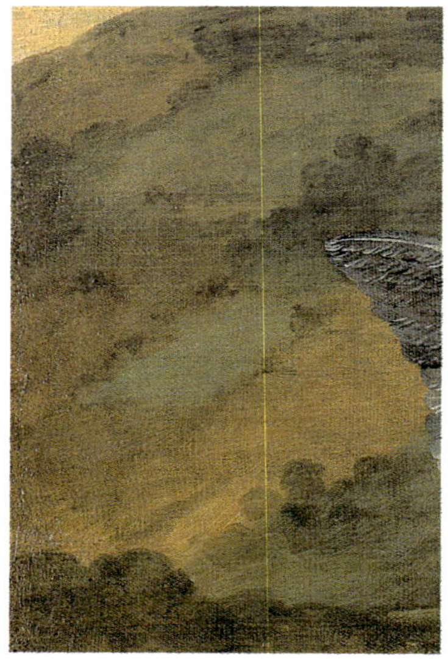

Even the formal eighteenth-century portrait can include moments of brilliant abstraction, as opposite, where white on white calligraphy emerges from the surrounding browns like a milky flower or a silent galactic explosion. Painting the cravat of his sitter gave the virtuoso artist an area of free-play, an indulgence in the pleasure of paint.[2]

[1] Another term for it is non-referential art (sometimes non-figurative art). Kandinsky, Mondrian and Malevich were the pioneers of abstraction in the early years of this century.
[2] Sir Thomas Lawrence. *Portrait of William Linley 1789* (p.27). The detail is roughly actual size.

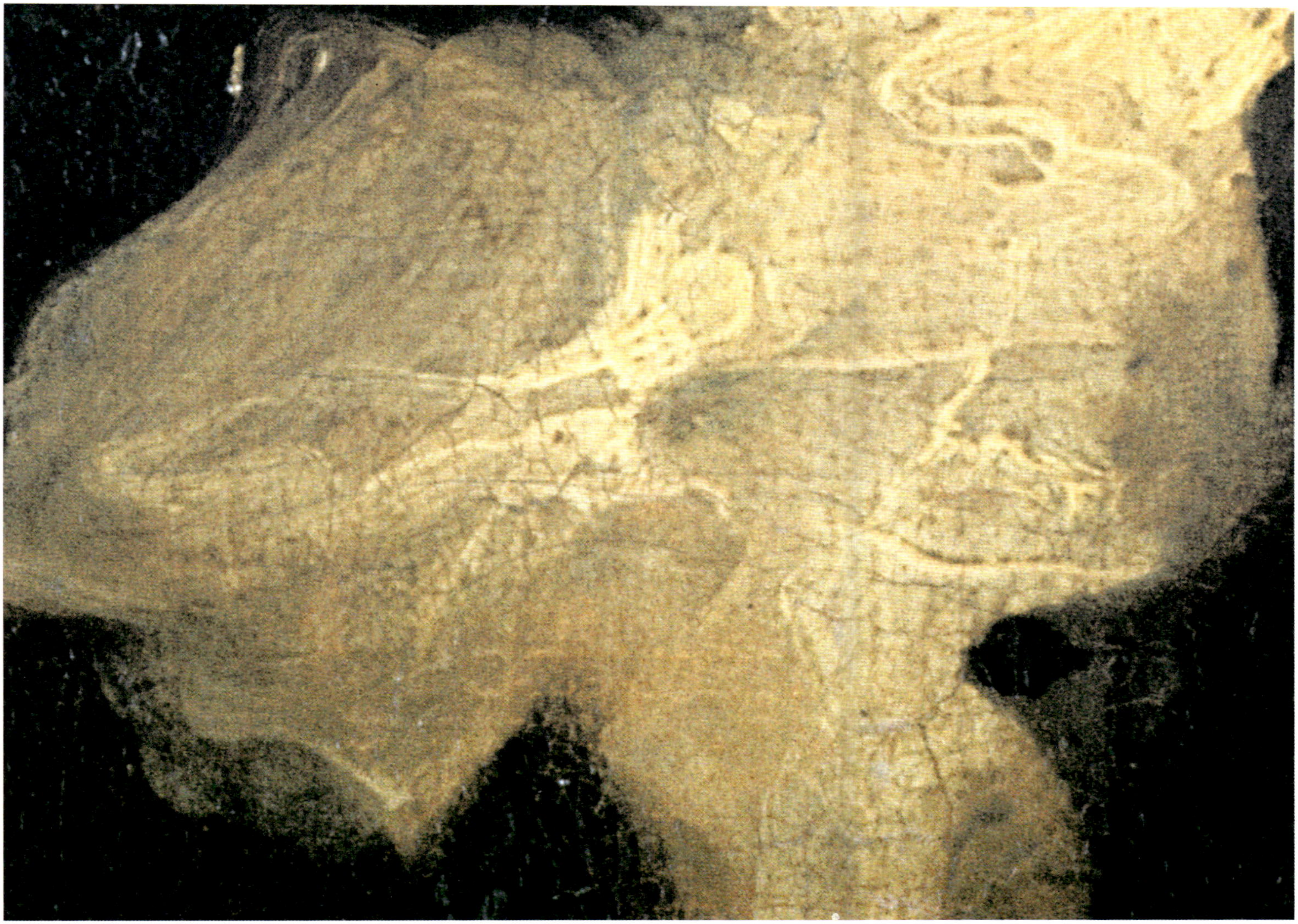

B is for Beauty

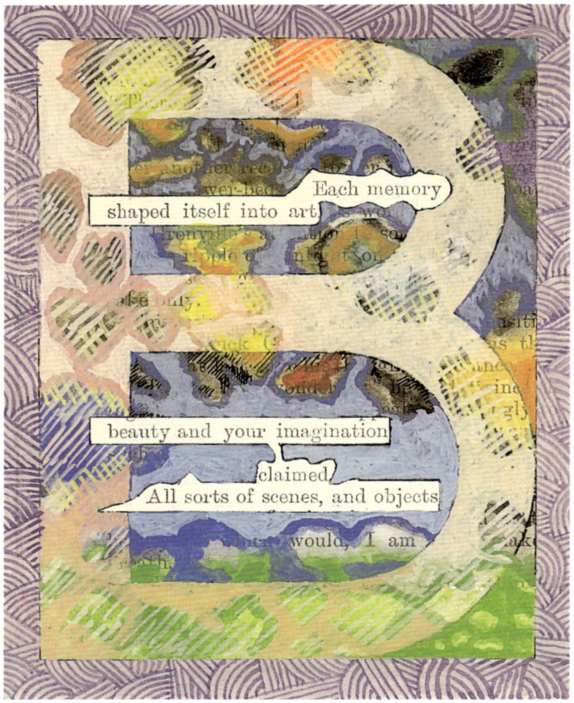

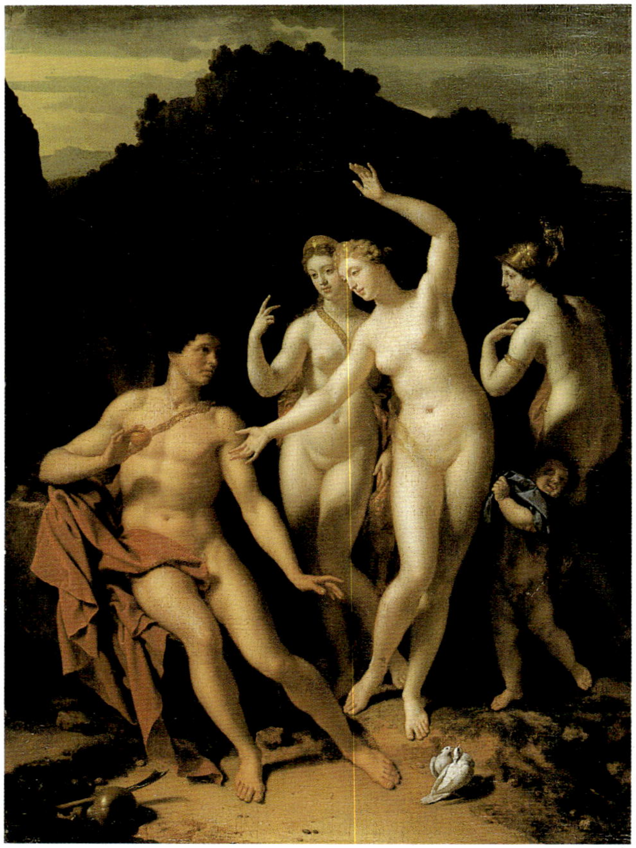

Art's job is to add to the world's store of beauty. This does not mean only to make beautiful things but even more importantly to increase the stock of things in which beauty can be seen. It has been the intense labour of artists over a thousand generations that has bequeathed to us the aspects of beauty we now take for granted: the magnificence of animals, the idea of visual delight in landscape (p.34), the pleasure in arrangements of objects (p.48), right up to the every-day accidentals of urban life.[1]

Although human beings are ultimately no more lovely than cockroaches or dandelions we are at pains to invest ourselves with a special beauty with gradations from the ugly to the divinely graceful. Painters and sculptors have long been on call to define and redefine these canons (a task now passed to photography and the cinema) and to shape the type of beauty fashionable in each age.

Beauty is about judgement and, as usual, Greek mythology shows us the prototype in the story of the Judgement of Paris;[2] a rigged contest like many a beauty competition since. Painters have always liked the subject as a suitably classical alibi (especially in repressive times) for painting the female nude. Van der Werff's contestants (plus of course Paris who himself should be the epitome of the ideal male physique) are not too far from current versions of bodily perfection, for all their affected poses (Venus seems permanently about to topple over).

Everything in the picture is desexualised. A cloth falls across the genitals of Paris, and the goddesses (as is the standard practice of classical statues) have had their pubic hair removed, yet the

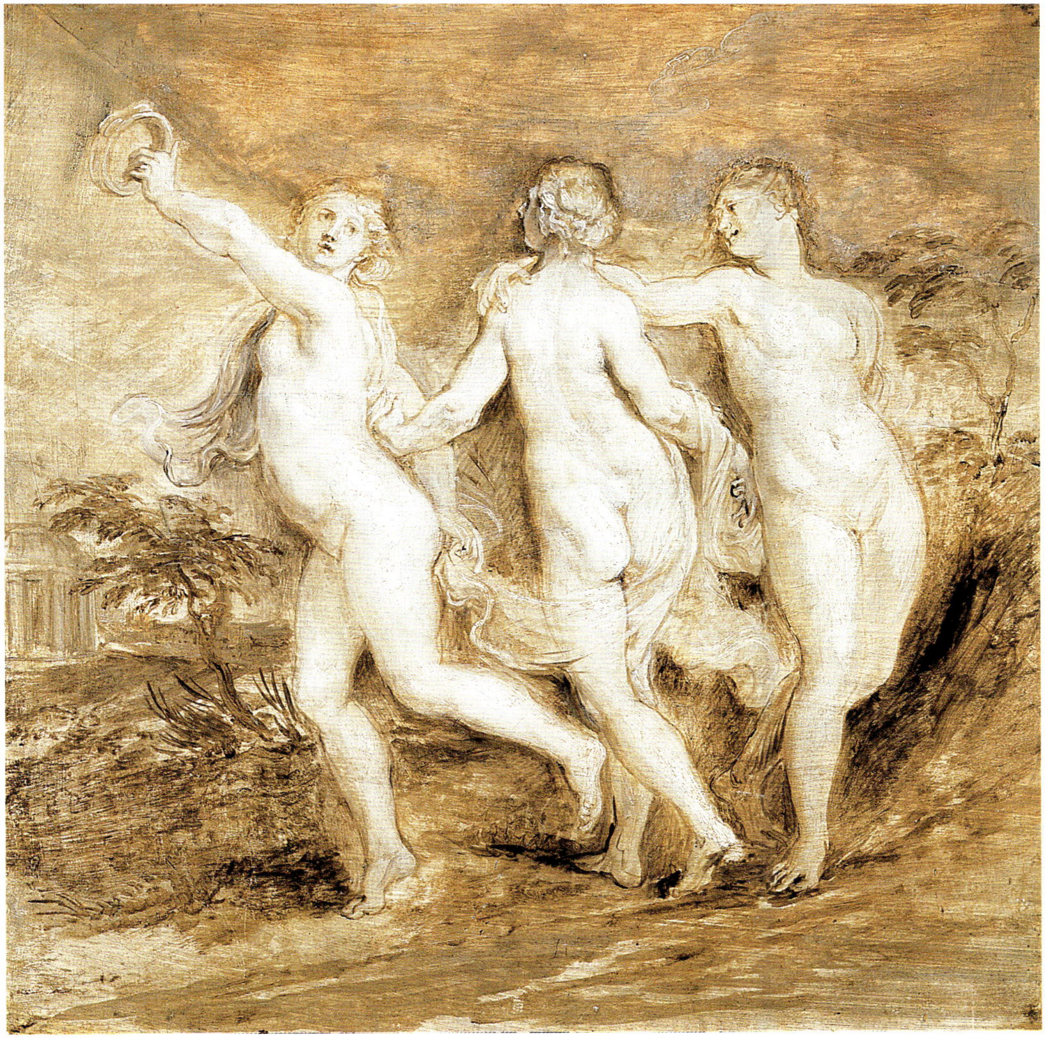

presence of erotic symbols helps the narrative (Cupid is there with his arrows of desire and two turtle doves are about to copulate in the foreground).

If this picture seems a chaos of arms and legs it is simply that Van der Werff is rather an incompetent painter and has not got his composition under control. There are beastly paintings about the beautiful just as there are beautiful paintings about the beast.

Rubens's women are physically a world apart, and their generous anatomy has not had a revival in this slimming-conscious age. These are real child-bearing women and not porcelain confections. In a couple of hours at the easel, Rubens has created a female trio infinitely more convincing than that which Van der Werff probably laboured on for weeks. If one of these or his own Venus (p.19) were to enter Van der Werff's insubstantial world their warm-blooded humanity would shatter it.

When beauty is the subject of a picture which is in itself striving for beauty the problem is compounded, as in Van der Werff's misunderstanding of the task, or enriched as with Rubens. In this larger context art has nowhere to hide, for it is not a passive spectator at beauty's parade but its producer, organiser and arbiter.

---

[1] A recent example is the scandal caused by the Tate Gallery's acquisition of Carl André's brick arrangement. Those who argued against a pile of bricks being art at all did not notice that their perception of such piles in their daily travels had been heightened and vivified. Art had thus fulfilled its obligations even while it was being scorned.

[2] An apple always spells trouble in mythology and fairy tales. This episode, full of bribes and an unrefusable offer to a young mortal (the undying love of the woman of his dreams), led to the Trojan war.

C is for Conservation

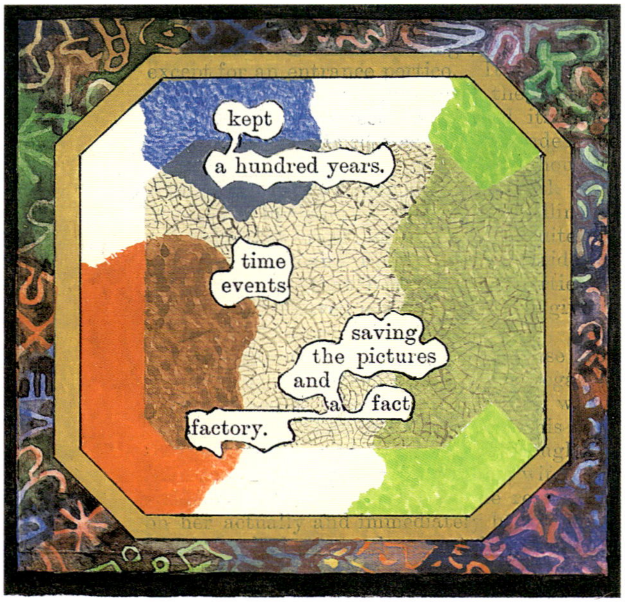

Galleries used merely to be places with pictures in them, but now the halls hung with paintings represent only a fragment of a museum's purpose. Behind them is a whole industry of conservation and scholarship. The technical sophistication of the former now calls for analysis, x-ray and a laboratory for chemical macrophotography. Things the painter himself would have forgotten that he did are revealed by radiography and colours that he used and covered over are shown in cross-sections of paint layers magnified, as here (in a tiny sample of Veronese's sky: see opposite) to approximately 750 times actual size. [1]

The background of scholarship is equally impressive. The books written on the artists in the collection would already fill a whole room. If you decided to read all the studies, catalogues and articles on Rembrandt you would have to spend longer doing it than it took Rembrandt to produce his oeuvre. Tap Poussin into the computer of an art history library and the list of relevant texts (which now includes the words you are reading) would scroll away for hours.

If only one could tell those dedicated artists of the past that battalions of paid people spend their whole lives thinking about them and their work. Or would perhaps the thought of such eternal scrutiny paralyse them? [2]

Art historians keep us on our toes by regularly changing the labels on pictures. What was once 'by x' is modified to 'studio of x', which suggests that 'x' had a hand in its design, but that it was executed by assistants. A little more doubt enters in and the painting is further demoted to 'circle of x' or 'follower of x', which means that 'x' had nothing to do with it except that his style exerted a strong influence and attracted imitations.

The Veronese here (see opposite before restoration) would continue to be a mystery were it not for such labours. In 1948 it was cleaned to reveal elements such as a disembodied hand holding a pair of scales, which confirmed that it was a fragment of a large altarpiece described in old documents. The picture had been cut up in the eighteenth century in order to sell it as three more conveniently sized items.[3] The other two surviving pieces were traced to Edinburgh and Ottawa. Putting all three together shows that the central figure is missing and, presumably, (since armless Saint Michaels are not sought after) destroyed. The 'complete' version (overleaf, p.14) is only my conjecture based on previous suppositions by experts.

Thus enjoyment, interest and authenticity are enhanced by the sleuths of scholarship and the conscientious vigilantes of conservation.

[1] A small cross-section of paint layers in the dark blue area of sky. The bottom layer is the primer now discoloured from its original white to brownish-yellow. A layer of lead white mixed with azurite lies on top of this and a thicker layer, with more particles of azurite, on top of that. The lighter blue underneath gives luminosity to the final darker layer.

[2] It's difficult to imagine that Poussin, whose work was seen by only a handful of people in his lifetime, would not be pleased to know that three hundred years later an exhibition of his paintings at the Royal Academy attracted 200,000 visitors.

[3] It is safe to say that the inconvenient bits of cloak and devil etc. were painted over to deceive the client into thinking he had a complete Veronese. The now shadowy lion was also removed although a knowledgeable buyer would expect Saint Jerome (who is easily identified as a founder of the church from the miniature example he holds) to be accompanied by the usual peaceable beast.

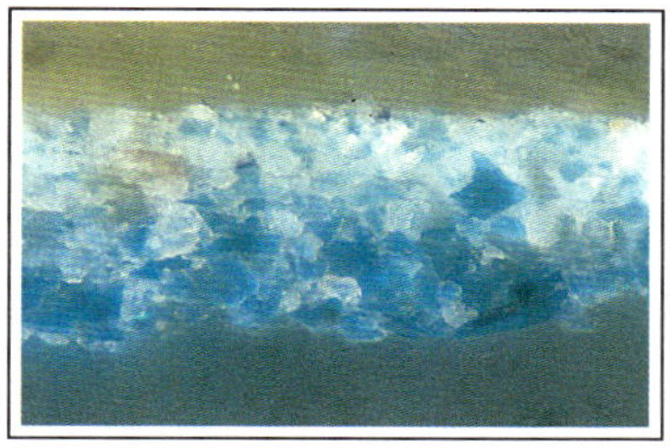

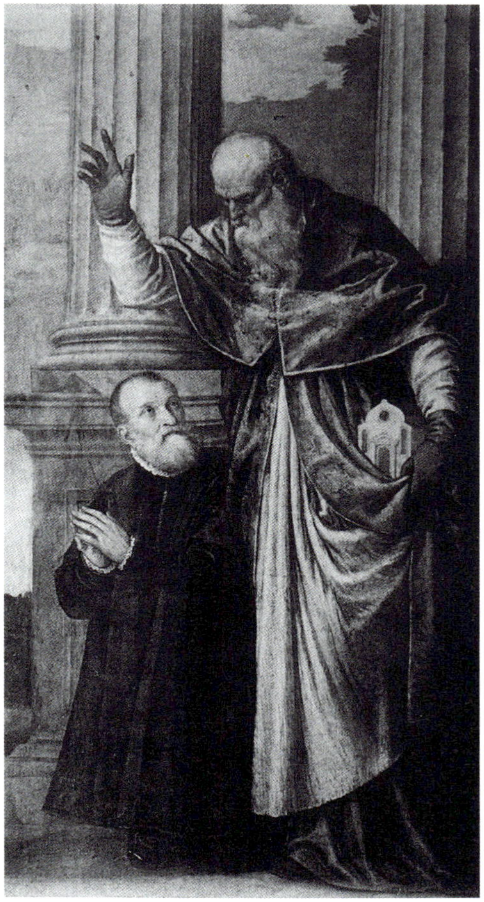

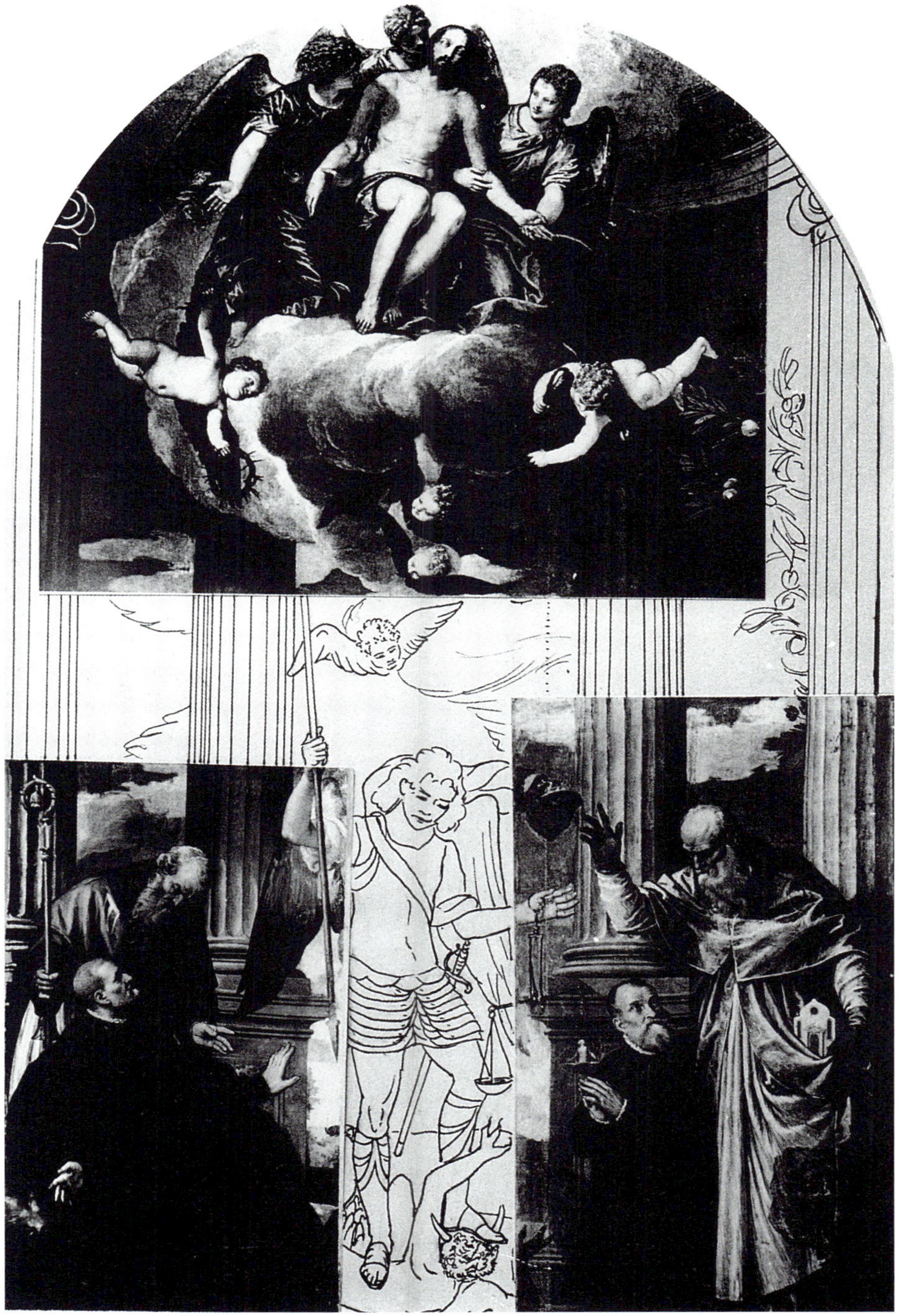

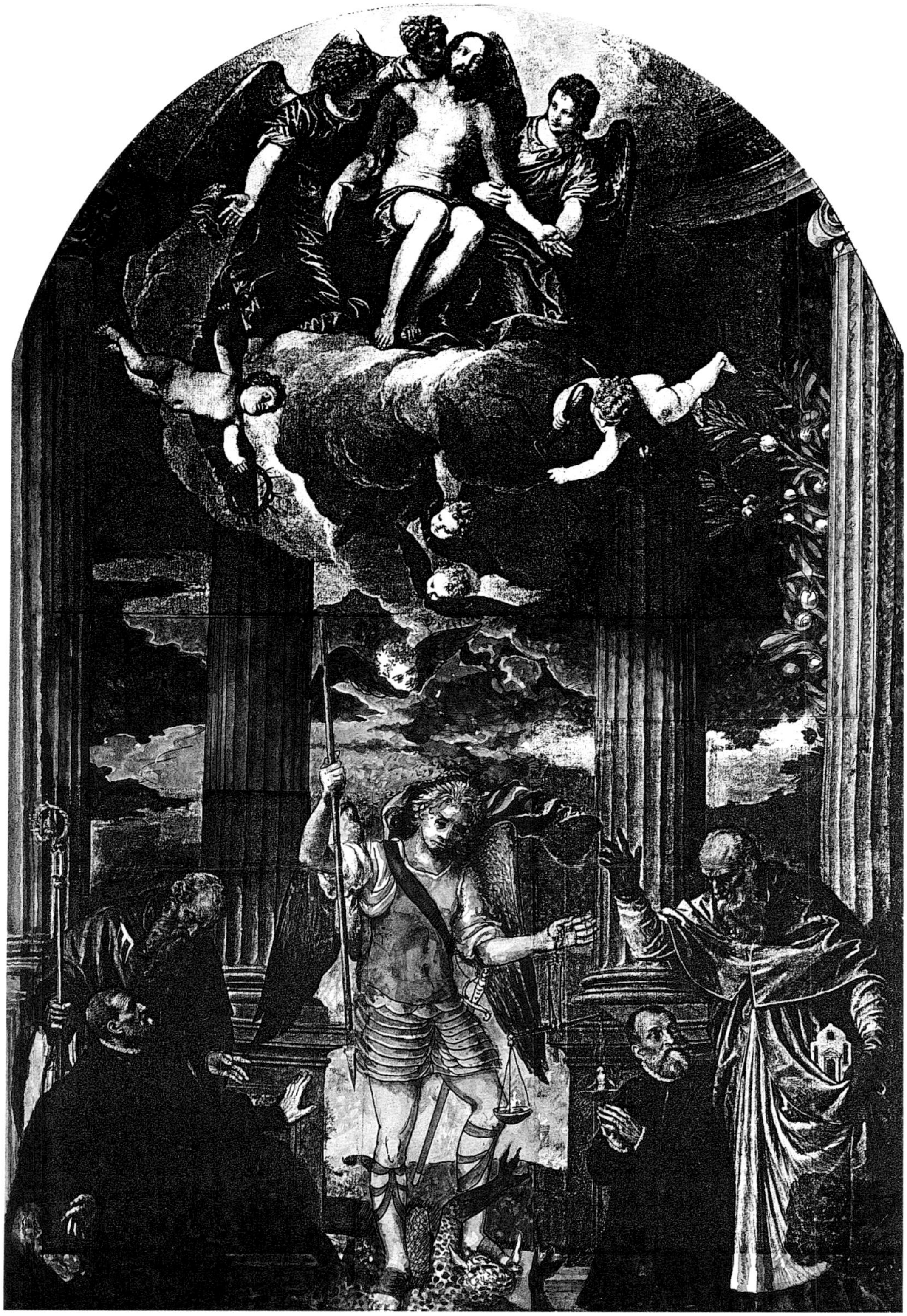

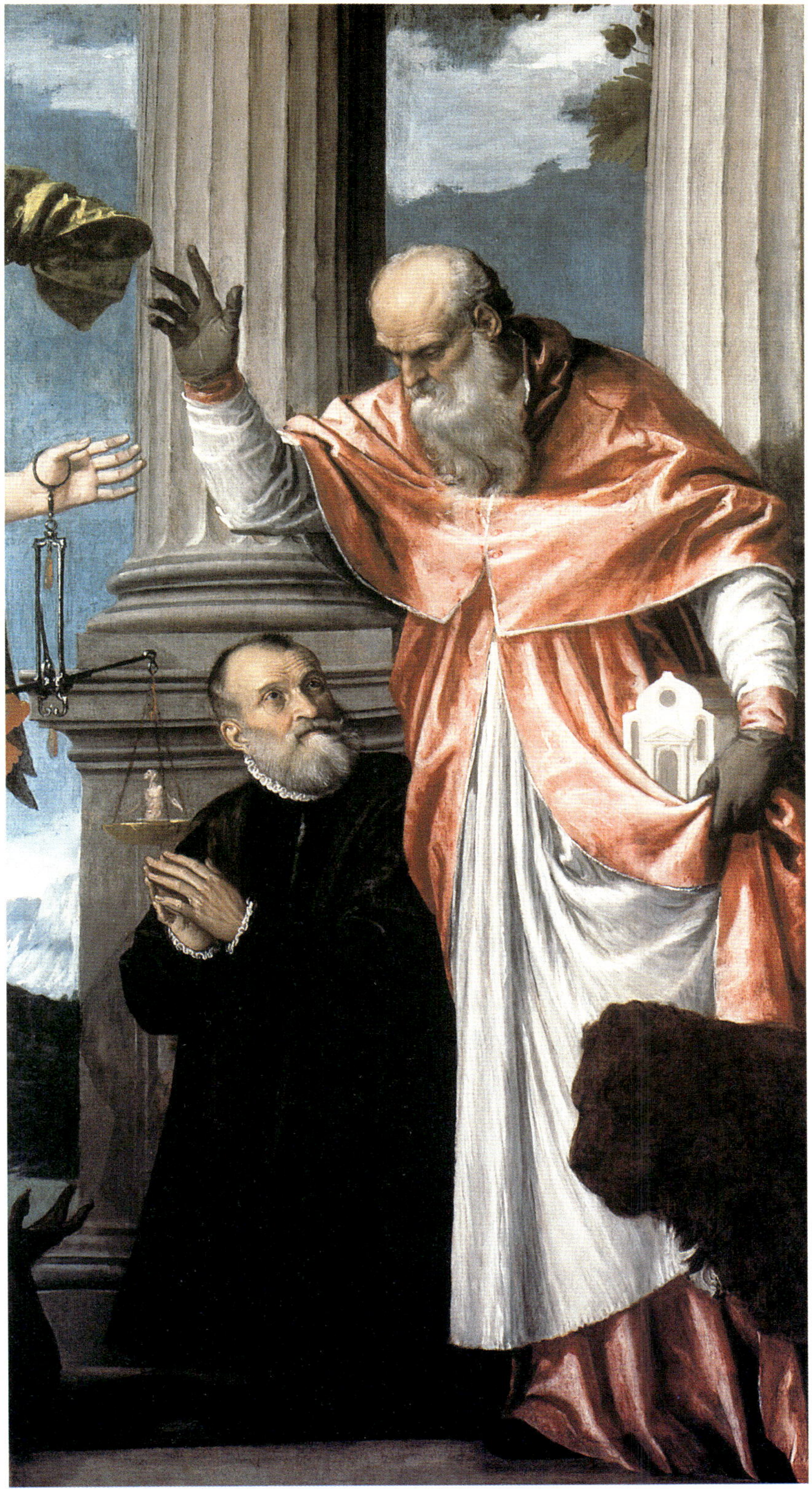

D is for Detail

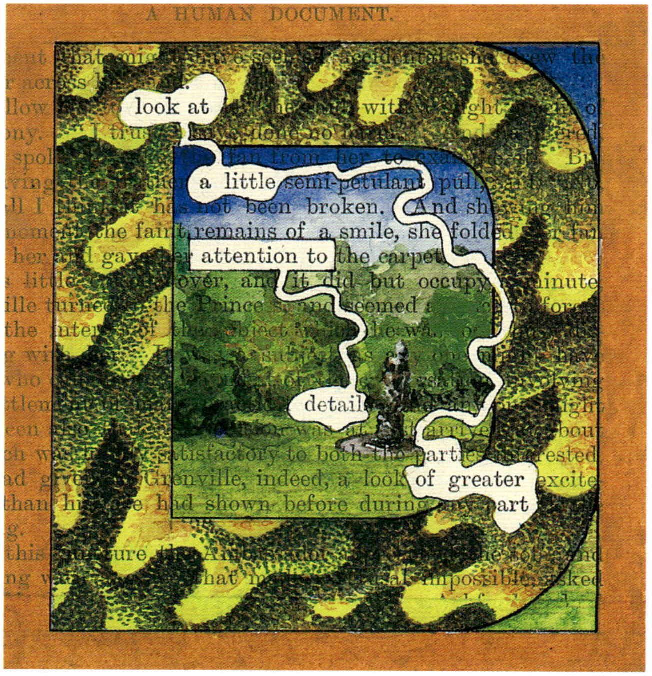

How detailed can pictures ultimately be? Nature of course is infinitely examinable: one can carry on enlarging any fragment of it for ever until one is looking at the atomic structure of the thing itself with an electron microscope. Pictures, however detailed they seem to be (like the van Huysum, p.33), are always generalisations of some kind. What seems an illusionistic landscape will let you down in the end, however you may claim that you can 'count every blade of grass'. You look for the individual tree and the separate leaf on the tree and then the veins on that particular leaf. Somewhere along this line of looking, art will break down. There is a point in any painting where everything becomes just paint, and, however fascinating macrophotographs of paint layers are to the specialist (and useful to the art historian, p.13) they tell us nothing about what *art* is made of. Views of microscopic bits of pigment are just as interesting when they come from very bad pictures as when they are taken from masterpieces.

Luckily this makes finickiness irrelevant to the quality of a work of art. Some of the most obsessively detailed paintings that exist have been painted by inmates of mental institutions.[1]

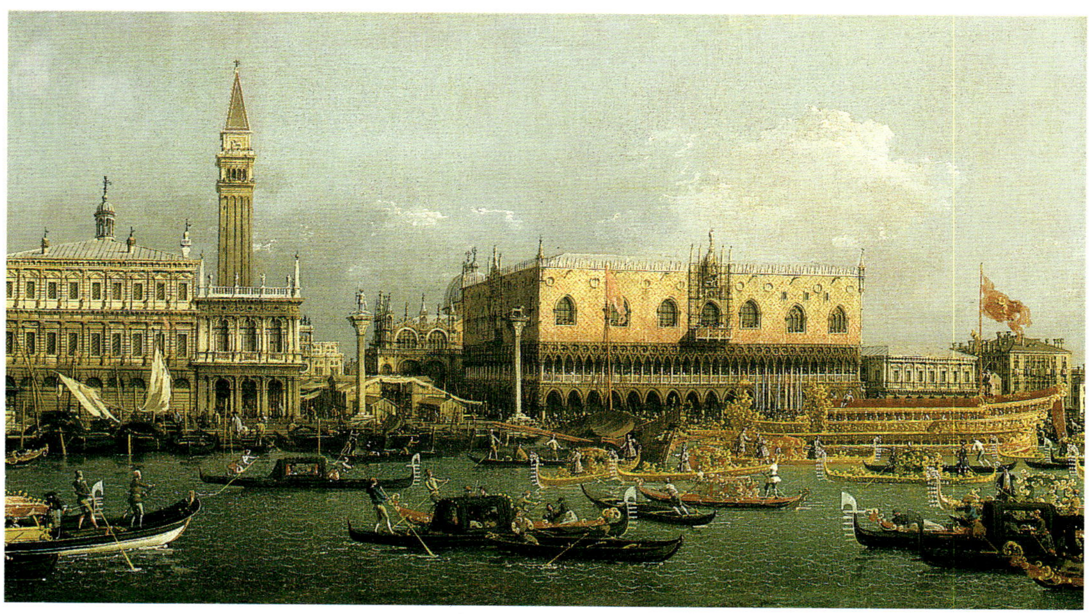

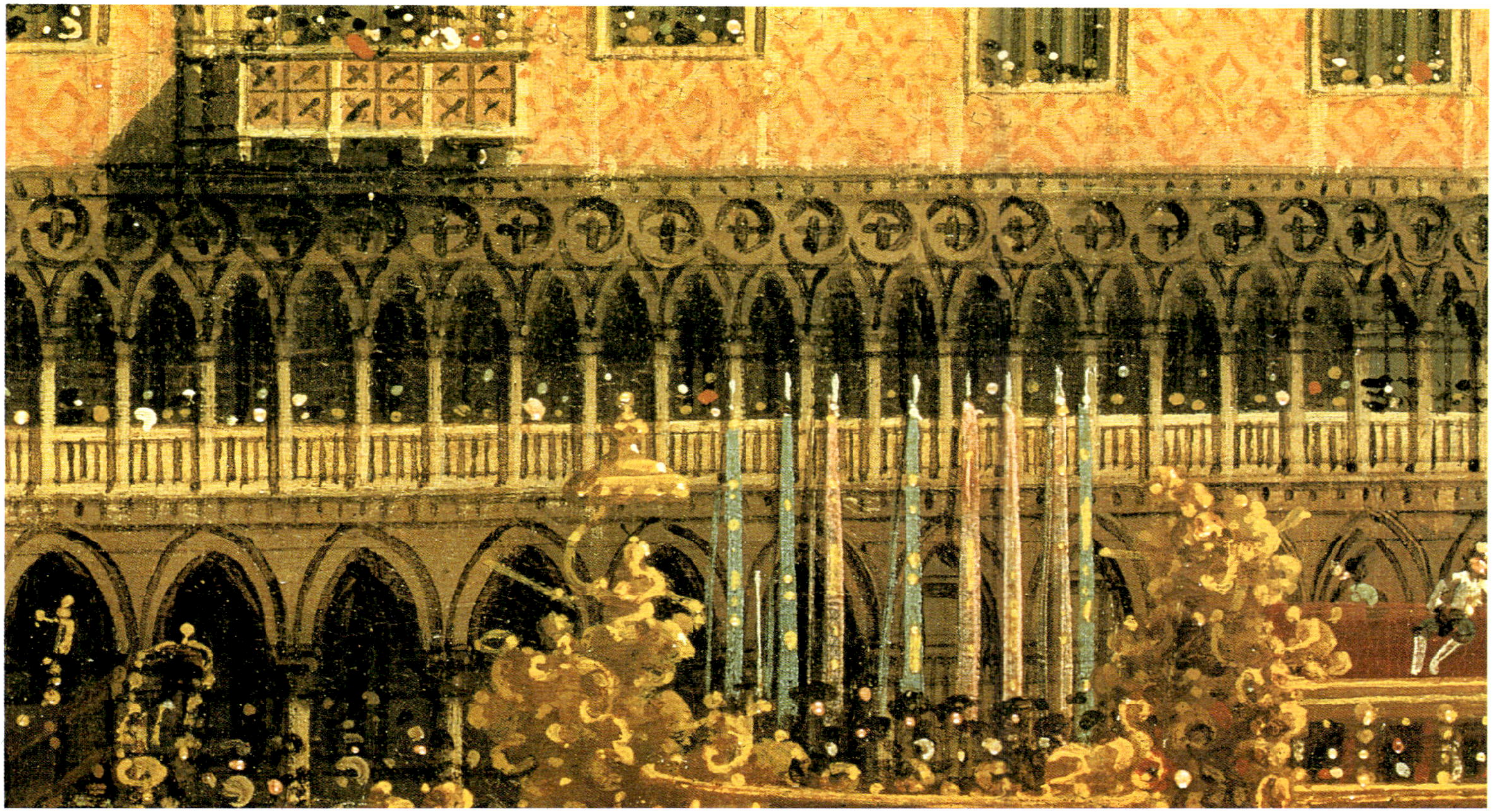

The group of people on this spectacular balcony are imagined by us from a schema provided with practiced virtuosity by Canaletto, for whom a handful of well-crafted dots suffice to conjure up a world. Looking at the picture from a distance we are in no doubt that the balcony is amply peopled. Moving in close we realise how much work *we* put in and how simple was the artist's strategy that persuaded us to supply the figures and the animation of their lives.

Canaletto was particularly adept at such tricks having worked as a youth in his father's scene-painting shop where flats and backdrops were done at great speed solely to be read from a distance by a theatre audience. [2] The more you look at his paintings the more they seem schematised: the artist has found ways of writing figures, has discovered the signs for various parts of buildings and the calligraphy of landscape and water. [3] The result is amazingly convincing, although the process is as 'naturalistic' as morse code.

The greatest painters of apparent detail are all in their different ways illusionists (Gainsborough, p.47). The silks shine, brocades glisten, lace and ribbons are infinitely complicated in their folds and knots until you get up close when there is often nothing to see at all but a series of rapid scribbles and swipes of the brush. What takes the time is learning how little is needed to suggest the world to eyes that know it.

[1] Often of course these are also of high quality but they somehow lie beyond the bounds of communicative expression, locked as they tend to be in some obsessive maze. Now usually referred to by the useful term 'Outsider Art' such work already has a museum and a literature devoted to it.

[2] This speed of performance was a great asset to Canaletto in what was virtually a factory for Venetian views. He was supplying the great stream of visitors on the Grand Tour who had a taste for such superior souvenirs. Eventually one hung in almost every English stately home.

[3] The other (and finer) Canaletto in the gallery, a view of old Walton Bridge on the Thames, does not have this factory-made look. It is a painting made for a discerning patron of the artist and not for the tourist market.

E is for Education

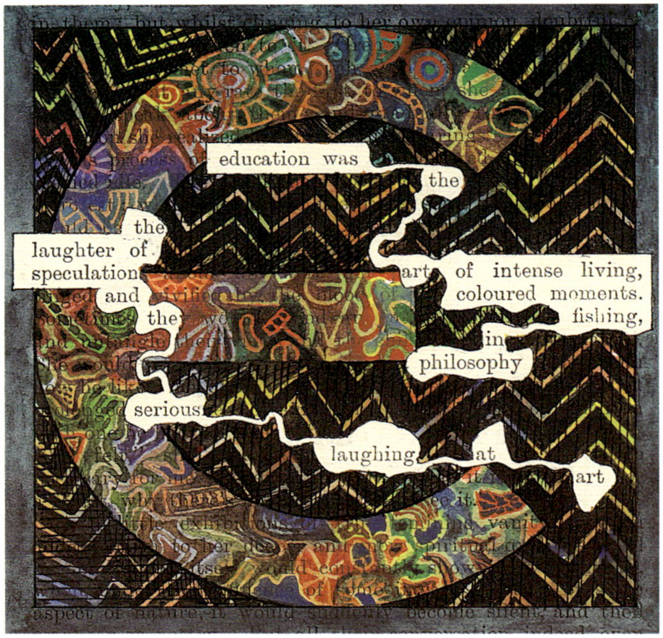

Looking at art is a primary experience and therefore, fortunately, not educational at all. Facts about paintings and their artists, dates and accounts of their iconography (what the things in an image mean) can all be part of education but the pictures remain art: their qualities as such make them inviolable. A bad picture contains as much information as a good one, just as a clock that does not work is as intricate as one that does.

The Bamana of Mali have no word for art (though they make superb sculpture) but have a phrase for special statues, 'things that can be looked at without end'. I know of no better definition of art.

It is one of the alibis of gallery-going that one will learn a lot. Yes, you can learn the orders of Venetian architecture from a Canaletto (he is, after all, inventing the idea of Venice for us) but the picture is not there for the purpose of teaching it.

If you love a painting you may well want to know its history, but you can equally learn all about it without its meaning anything to you (other than echoes of that knowledge rebounding off the painted surface). To admire, enjoy or love a masterpiece is already to have understood it. Education in that sense can be bypassed. A great painting is a cultural and not an educational object.

Perhaps the first artist whose culture was fluently international was Rubens. His comprehensive understanding moved easily in space and time. Just as he found it natural as a courtier and diplomat to be in Spain, Italy or England,[1] so he effortlessly assimilated the mythologies of the past and realised them in a language of the present.

The picture opposite shows a holy trinity of mother, father and child; namely Venus, Mars and their son, Cupid.[2] Rubens paints these deities as if he was on terms of familiarity with them. If on another easel there had been a corresponding trio from christian mythology (Joseph, Mary and the infant Jesus) the change of subject would have been marked by an appropriate shift of mood and manner: yet one could have seen immediately the unity of vision as one mythology is observed through the world of another.

There can be no more tender view of the god of war than this fond father, nor a more generous view of the goddess of love than this abundant mother. He knows peace as he sees his beloved give their child the milk of her breast, and she unselfishness. Only when we have absorbed the emotional intimacy of the scene do the true relationships behind it start to charge the image with mythological tension, as the old stories flood in. These gods (unlike the christian holy family) are worse behaved than most of us mortals: this, like many such moments of human life, is a brief interval of perfection, a short respite of calm in a sea of moral chaos. We have been disarmed of our learning by the sophisticated persuasiveness of the artist. What seemed to be a red curtain turns into a cloud of blood which has already stained the wings of the callous Cupid. Venus's motherhood masks her promiscuity and the Gorgon stares from the shield of Mars ready for remorseless war.

The painting, beautiful in execution, seductive in colour, inventive in composition, is low on education but infinitely rich in culture. The picture teaches but is not instructive: we are enriched by it but not in measurable benefits.

---

[1] Rubens came to England on a diplomatic mission. He was knighted and given a major commission to paint the still-surviving ceiling of the Banqueting House in Whitehall.

[2] Venus is shown here with the illegitimate offspring of Mars, her husband's brother and her own half-brother; one of her many (often incestuous) liaisons. Cupid (Eros) was to wound his own mother with one of his arrows of love. Mars, as one might guess, spelled trouble wherever he was.

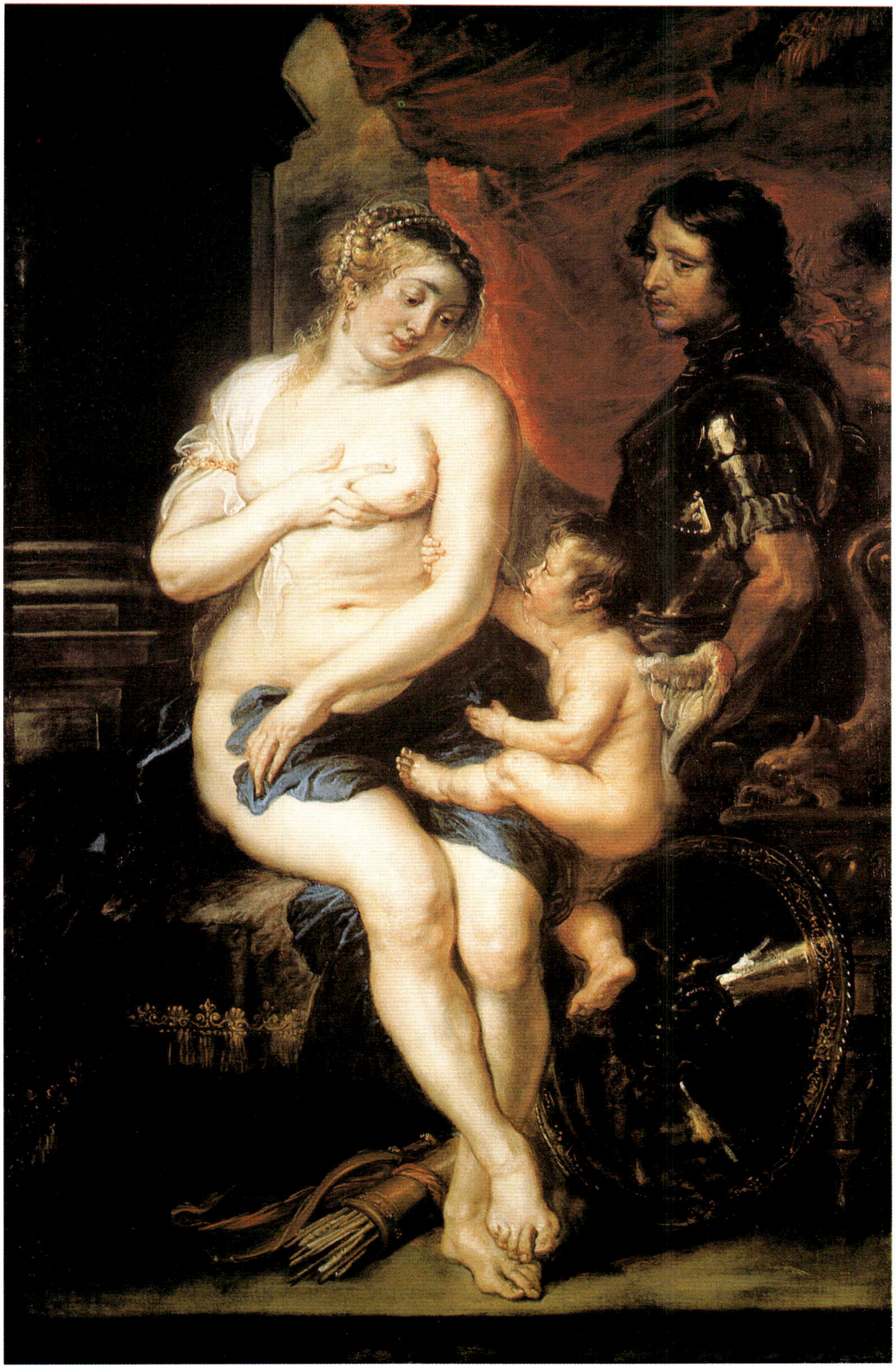

F is for Frame

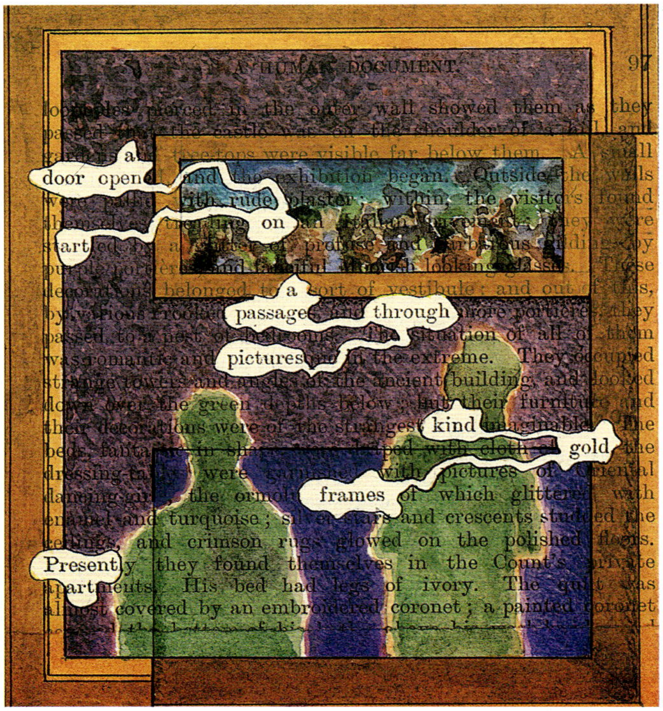

A sure way of upsetting an artist whose exhibition you have seen is to say that you liked the frames. The job of the frame is to draw attention to the picture rather than itself (except when its opulence serves to announce the owner's wealth). The frame tells you, as does the proscenium arch of a theatre, where a world begins and ends. It isolates that world from surrounding distractions (horrible wallpaper, neighbouring pictures etc.). Being palpably three-dimensional the frame asserts the flatness of the picture while, with its window-like structure, it increases the sense of depth which that flatness captures. Ideally this is done by stealth so that later on you cannot remember what the frame was like.

There are fashions in framing as in everything else, as can be seen in any art gallery where the pictures come from different periods. One age thinks that gold alone can be the answer and the more massive and ornate the better, and another reacts with wide black frames of varying degrees of severity: such catholic and protestant solutions persist to this day. Almost everyone has had the agonising experience of deciding how to frame some favourite image.

The picture opposite has three frames which should, one might suppose, act like a triple fanfare to announce some central wonder. The reverse is in fact the case since the climactic middle to which your attention is so emphatically drawn is a dismal affair. Not only are there three frames but they are each by a different person. The first (not shown) is the serviceable work of the craftsman who framed the canvas. The second is a brilliant border of superbly painted flowers. The third and innermost frame is a clumsy mock-sculpted cartouche containing (by the same leaden hand) a feeble monochrome devotional scene. For all its laboured shading this ornamental border which is meant to produce a sensation of high relief is dull and lifeless. It is difficult to imagine that the pious Daniel Seghers [1] who painted the exquisite floral improvisation was such a specialised artist that he could not, in a couple of hours, have knocked off both a more convincing surround or a group (of the Virgin and Child with Saint Anne) less stiff and unimaginative than this awkward trio.

Apart from this image all the works reproduced in this book appear without frames: it would certainly look eccentric had it been otherwise. Curiously enough the margin of paper surrounding each of them provides a frame of the most unlikely colour. It would be difficult to imagine the Dulwich Picture Gallery with all its paintings in brilliant white frames, yet we have learned to accept this convention in books. The ideal frame is perhaps a black room in which only the picture is illuminated. Only thus would the problem of conflicting light sources be eliminated.[2] If we see, in a gallery lit from the right, a landscape in which the sun shines from the left, we have to fight harder to inhabit it with our imagination.

---

[1] Seghers was a pupil of Jan Bruegel the elder and became a devout member of the Jesuits for whom his popular and highly-priced flower pictures earned a fortune.

[2] A cheaper way of achieving something of this effect is by looking at pictures through a dark tube (even a rolled up magazine will do) held very close to one eye (with the other eye shut). Look at any part of a picture through this so that you can see none of the edges of the painting. Suddenly you are in the painter's own world sharing his own experience or vision of light. The absence of conflicting information is akin to the painter's absorption in his subject. New depths emerge and a heightened awareness of space and atmosphere. As soon as a bit of the frame or wall comes into sight the illusion vanishes. To a limited extent this can work with reproductions of a reasonable size, but in a gallery the sensation can be peculiarly intense.

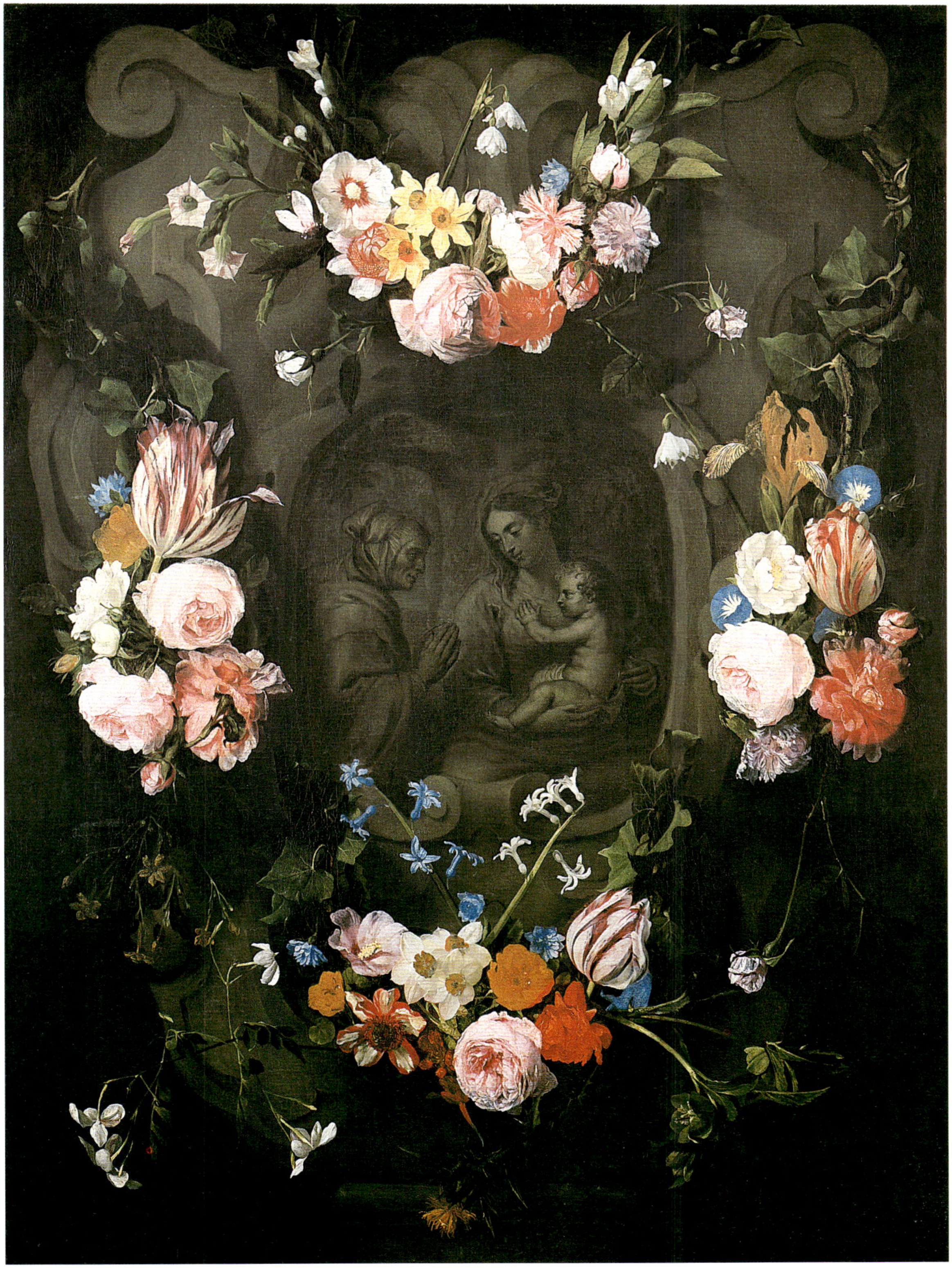

G is for Grammar

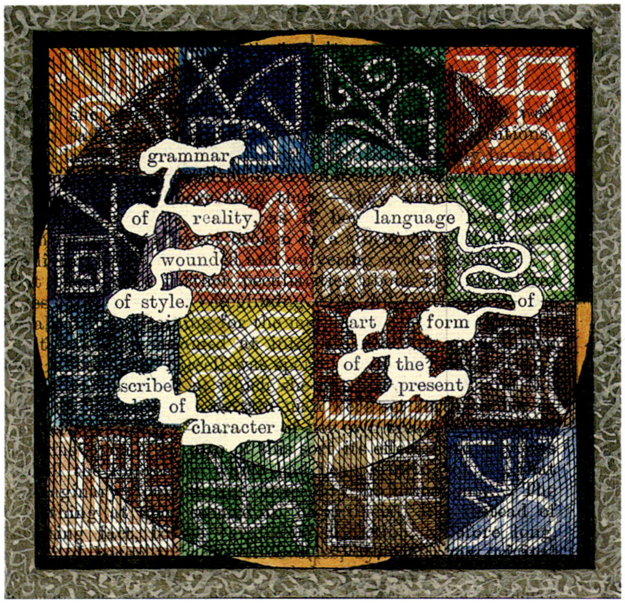

Just as language has a grammar to determine its structure and the relationship of its various parts, so painting has a schematic basis to give it coherence. Some kinds of image-making in the past have had a grammar so rigid that the pictorial language remained constant for hundreds of years. Egyptian painting is the extreme example, though there are long and unchanging schools of ikon makers. For them what had been done became what must be done. This applied to every aspect of the picture so that the colour of this god's beard or that saint's clothes were as fixed as the proportions and positions of their bodies.

Western painting in general is not so rule-bound, yet there are grammatical ways of thinking about colour and the disposition of light and dark on the surface, as well as that semi-invisible scaffolding that holds pictures together. The uniform practice (that developed out of growing literacy) of making paintings, like pages, read from left to right [1] is a self-reinforcing habit that can be exploited in different ways (p.25).

The idea of the rectangle as a generally agreed format (plus occasional visits to related shapes with rectangular implications such as the circle and the oval) was early established when paintings became portable objects. The bare rectangle itself has a grammar in that there are ideal formats that painters have come to prefer and in some cases hold sacred like the Golden Section

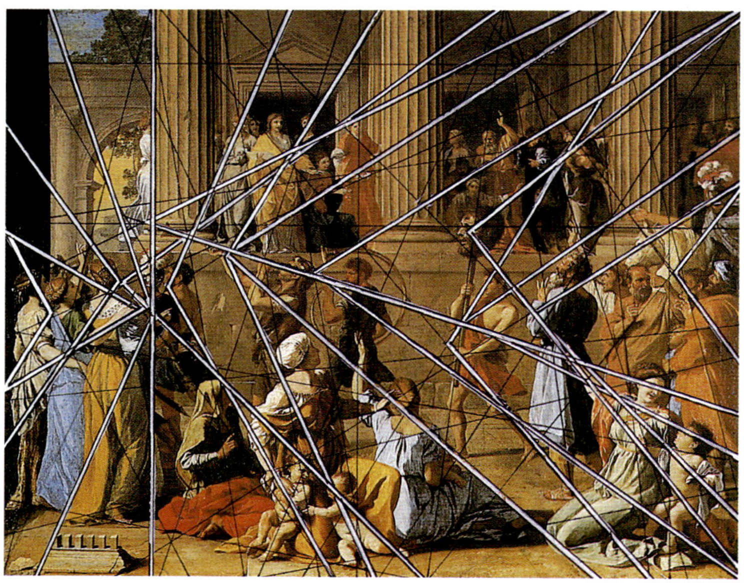

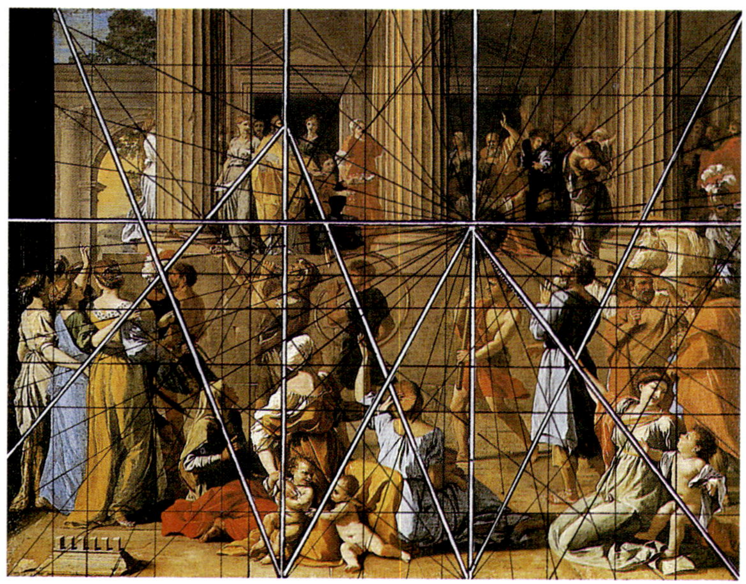

rectangle,[2] which can be seen to derive from natural growth patterns (as in the spiralling of a shell) and to obey the systems of ideal proportions of the ancient Greeks.

Once these proportions enter the orthodoxy the rectangle can be subdivided again and again to generate a network which the image can use as a guide. Some painters adhere to this principle with devotion,[3] while others achieve similar results by instinct.

Poussin, who imagined some lost Golden Age of painting whose rules would, as rhyme does for poets, set him free, is one of the great grammatical masters. One can take any of his paintings and analyse it for its grid of corresponding intersections and find that every important junction falls at an emphatic point in the picture. In slavish hands this can be a dull and mechanical procedure but in the hands of a genius (again, like rhyme and regular metre) it can lead to brilliant inventions.

Poussin's *Triumph of David* is the exemplary masterpiece of this. Within a horizontal and vertical grid deriving from the Classical architecture (which the returning David would have been surprised to see) the artist plays a dazzling game sending the exploring eye of the observer on many expeditions, so that each part of the canvas is visited and one is left with the vibrant experience of participation.

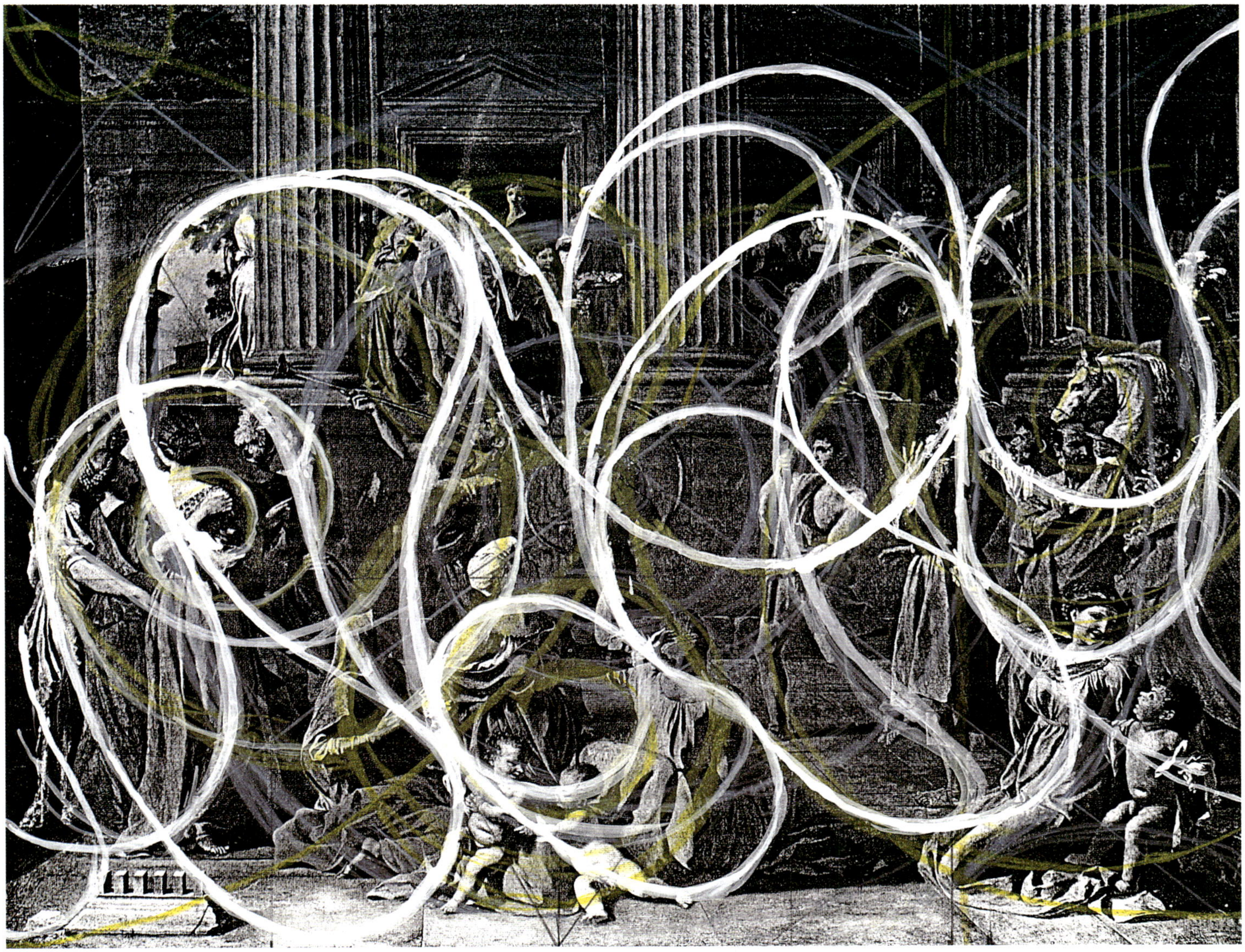

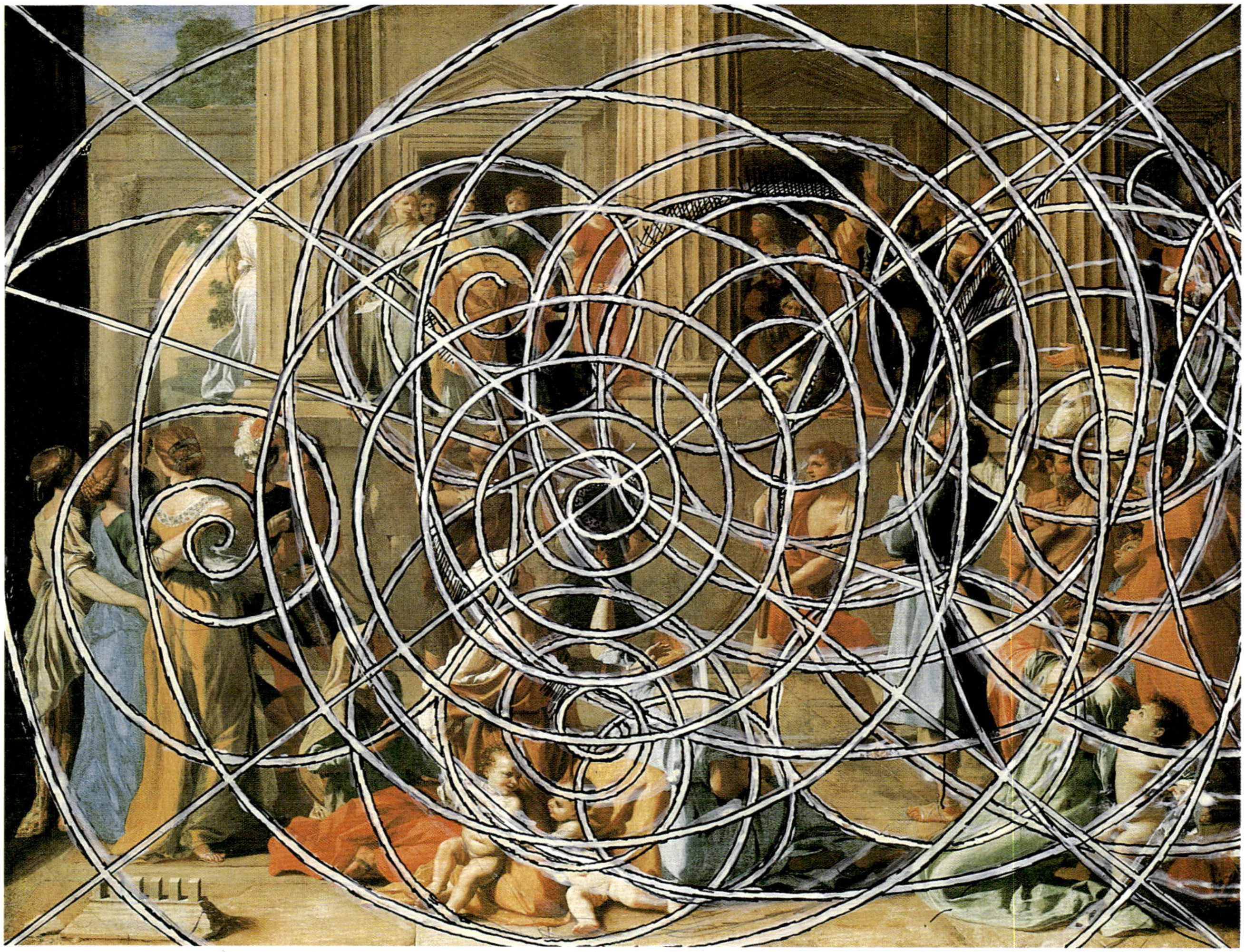

The eye is encouraged at the far left of the painting to make its usual journey towards the right hand edge of the picture. What it meets as it travels is a procession vigorously coming the other way: it is this conflict of a habit of looking with the nature of the event that sets up the initial energetic tension of the picture as powerful arrows of directional energy are encountered across the whole surface. The most traditional element of compositional grammar is also present in all innocence. Exactly where the climax of the event should be it is found. The head of Goliath which the procession is all about and to which all eyes turn is on the right of the image with its crucial wound positioned on the intersection of the two Golden Section divisions at the sides of the rectangle.

But this is not the only set of movements that the artist generates to keep the picture restless and invigorating. If the eye has persevered to the far right of the picture it is sent back along those same waves to the head of Goliath, from whose wound a spiral movement starts that carries one round the picture in a different direction. This in turn connects with other spirals most of which cross the central point of the canvas. This itself (starting at the mouth of the curved horn of victory) is the beginning of the large general spiral that encompasses the whole composition, as if it carried the reverberating sound to the edges and beyond.

This combination of rectilinear scaffolding and spiralling catherine wheels of composition is not the whole story but almost enough to show the mechanics of the picture as if one were drawing the inside workings of an intricate machine. Other structures can be found by following the use of colour as one can see from the perfect placing at intervals of the blue and red elements

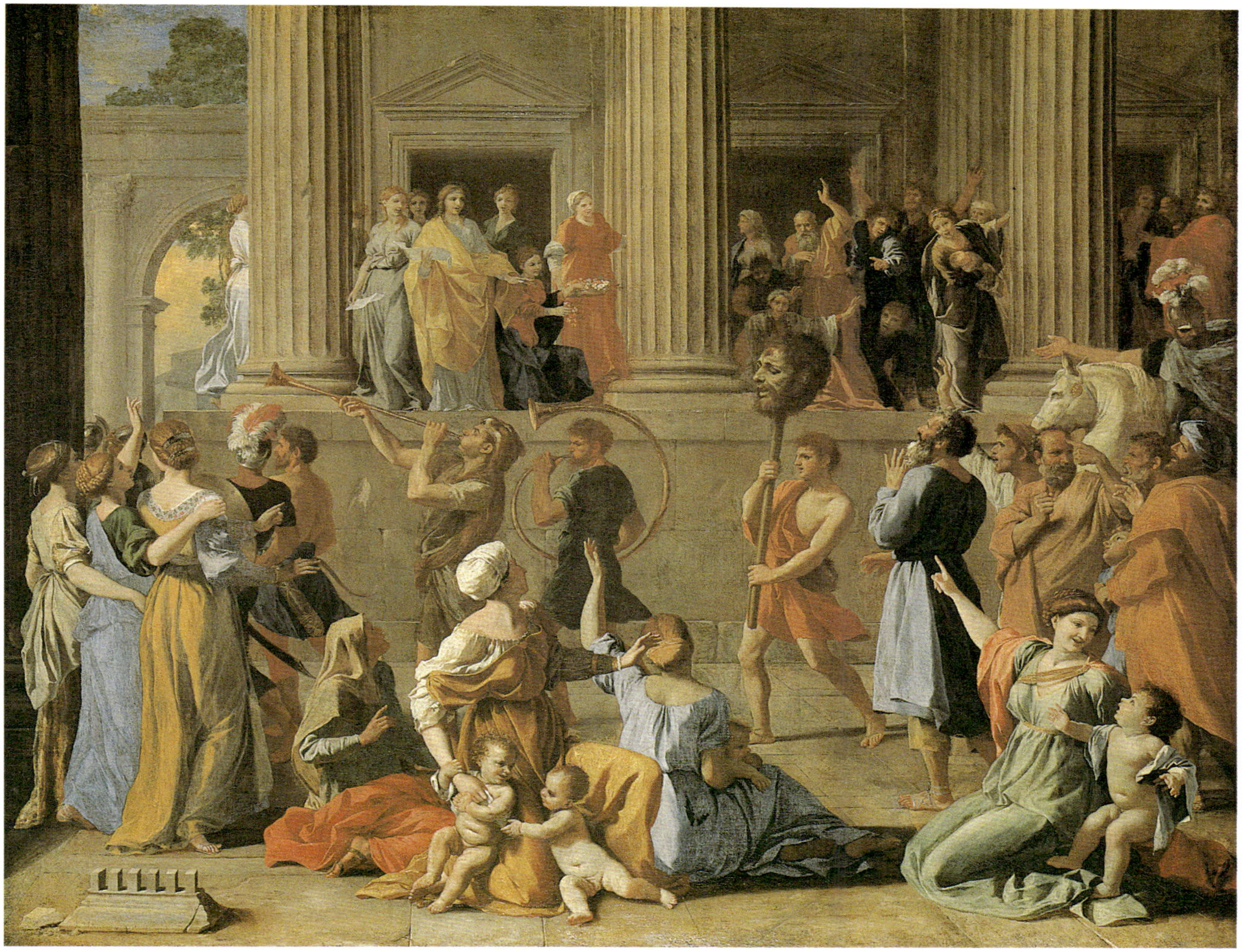

each of which sets up its own rhythm.

In music all this would be called counterpoint (as opposed to the harmony established by the colour) where one rhythmic structure supports and interlocks with another. If one seeks melody as well it is found in the more lyrical linear movement of the composition as a whole, a far from rigid fugue of ascending curves which have a voluptuous sprung formation as they move across. (see illustration p.23).

Poussin has pulled out all the grammatical stops to paint this small epic and used every device of his trade to produce the symphonic result. Yet as in the equally complex structures of Bach or Beethoven all is in the service of, and works to illuminate, a humanistic and poetic vision.

[1] It is for this reason that western eyes are flummoxed by oriental paintings. Our left-right reading habit drives us across the middle, say, of a Chinese painting and often passes through the area of least interest in a picture which in fact reads from top to bottom. Oriental and western eyes alike have difficulty in reading the works of cave artists and those from pre-literate societies for which neither of their reading practices is relevant or useful.

[2] The Golden Section is the point on a line where the shorter part is in proportion to the longer part as the longer part is to the whole line.

A C B

C is the Golden Section point. CB is to AC as AC is to AB. A perfect Golden Section rectangle is made with one side length AB and the other length AC. The proportions of a canvas roughly 80cm long and 50cm high.

[3] Notably Piero della Francesca who seems in the end to have abandoned painting for mathematics.

H is for Hazard/*A Humument*

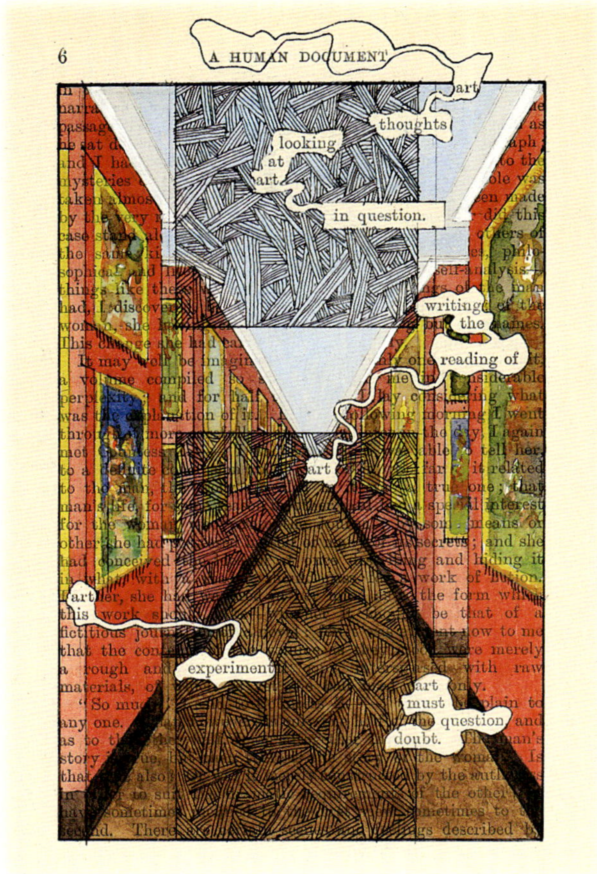

Hazard is a lovely word brought over by the Crusaders, the Arabic for risk and chance, luck and gaming dice (*al-zahr*). Chance and risk are at the heart of the artistic enterprise and nothing worthwhile can be made without inviting them to the feast. Hazard comes unbidden at the start since where an artist is born (and when and in what circumstances) will condition his art. It governs also whom he meets and by whom he is first taught. Before he has started to take over his own life and control his own career, hazard has already more than half formed him. It is at this point that the artist, who must guard and retain the child in himself, can decide to welcome chance as an active participant in his work just as he must embrace risk as the main force of change in what he does. Hazard starts as his prison and ends as his freedom.

The Dulwich Picture Gallery itself and the treasures it houses are the result of a sequence of chances and coincidences starting with an actor who knew Shakespeare and involving a collection destined for a Polish King, a Balzacian obsessive and his friend with their horde of pictures, and the Linleys, the most gifted dynasty in the history of English music, all in a cast of families and connections which, linked by the gallery, could form the basis of a costume epic cum soap opera stretching over the centuries.

Some coordinates on the web of hazard are also responsible for this book and the form it takes. The first is that I was born in Clapham and that when I was at school Dulwich was the nearest place to cycle where I could see great pictures. I have known these paintings virtually all my life, although, as in every fine collection, there are always new surprises, 'sleepers' like the Judd Memorial (p.49) which I seemed to have noticed only this year.

Another encounter with chance leads to the initials that divide and unite this book. This time hazard was deliberately invoked for, half my life ago, I decided to make an extended work based on the first book I could purchase for threepence. This, bought in a furniture repository on Peckham Rye (opposite the spot where William Blake saw his first angels), turned out to be Mallock's *A Human Document*, a once popular Victorian romance. I started to isolate little poems and phrases, drawing or painting over what was left, in December 1966. By 1970 I embarked on publishing these treated pages and in 1973 finished all 367 of them, at which point I started all over again. In each subsequent edition I replaced a group of pages with the intention of reaching one day (still far in the future) a final edition of *A Humument*[1] (as I called my work by conflating the original title), which would be the same book informed by the same idea and process but with no pages in common with the initial edition.

This alphabet is another of the many workings of the volume[2] which is pressed into service every time I have need to find new texts or to provide the design for posters, CD covers etc. The book has never let me down. Its vocabulary is large and I have never thought a thought I could not express through its words (with occasional recourse to parts of words, as so often here where 'art' is a part of 'part' etc.).

Nothing is so satisfying in art as finding a task that lasts for ever and in *A Humument* I've chanced upon exactly that. On their grander scale many of the pictures in this book are fragments of life-long quests, some involving great risks like the career of Rembrandt and others calling for exacting programs of research like that of Poussin. All were victims and beneficiaries of chance.

One of the happiest of these accidents was the coming together in Bath of Gainsborough and the Linleys. Although the Linley family moved in artistic circles and might now and again commission other painters for their portraits, such as Thomas Lawrence (below, right) whose cravat is earlier quoted as an example of abstraction (p.9), their main allegiance was to Gainsborough (himself an addicted musician) who presents them to us most freshly. It was William who donated the family pictures to Dulwich, including that of his sisters (p.47) and that of his older brother Thomas (below) in his red coat and tricorn hat. This touching portrait has the misfortune to prove here that hazard is not always kind, for Thomas Linley the younger was a child prodigy both as a violinist and composer. He was killed in a silly boating accident at the age of twenty- two. Mozart, who of all people could spot the real thing in a very young musician, said of him that, had he lived he would have become 'one of the greatest ornaments of the musical world'.

[1] Starting life as a manuscript and passing through a private press version it is now approaching its third trade edition published by Thames and Hudson. News of its progress, together with the most recent pages, can be found at website http://wwwwolfenet.com./~duchamp

[2] It has been used for the libretto of an opera and the words for commissioned songs, for the gores of a globe and the cladding of a skull, as well as most recently the text for a sculpture in wire.

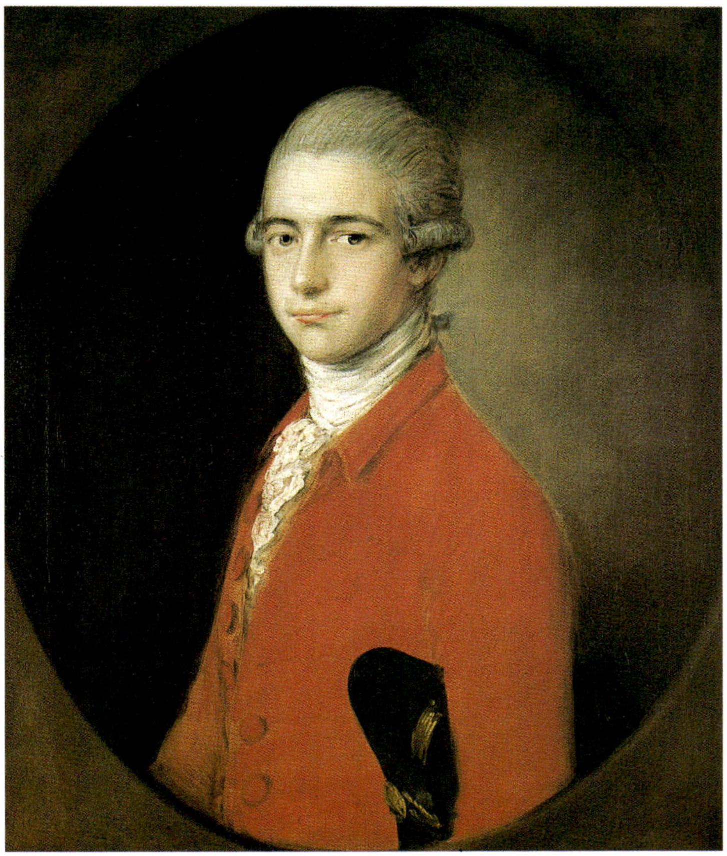

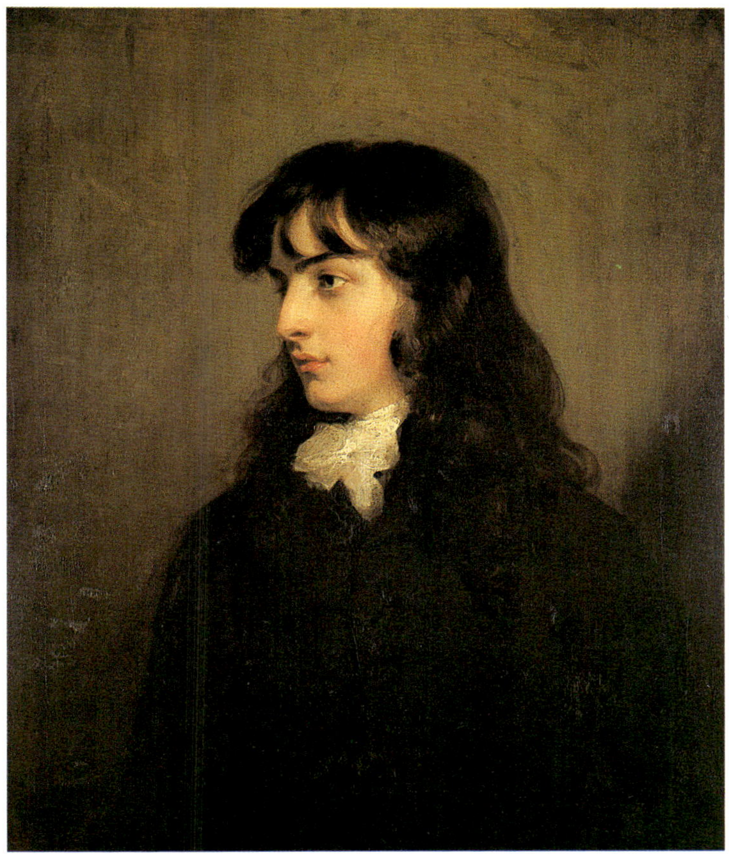

I is for Ism

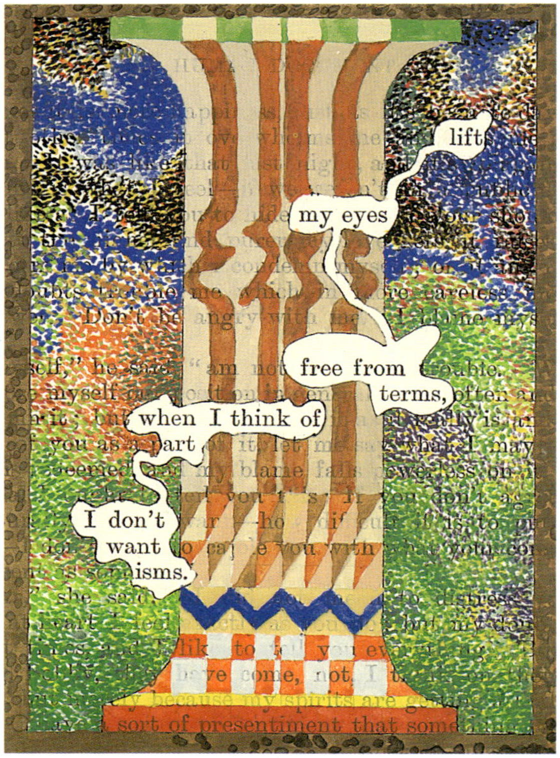

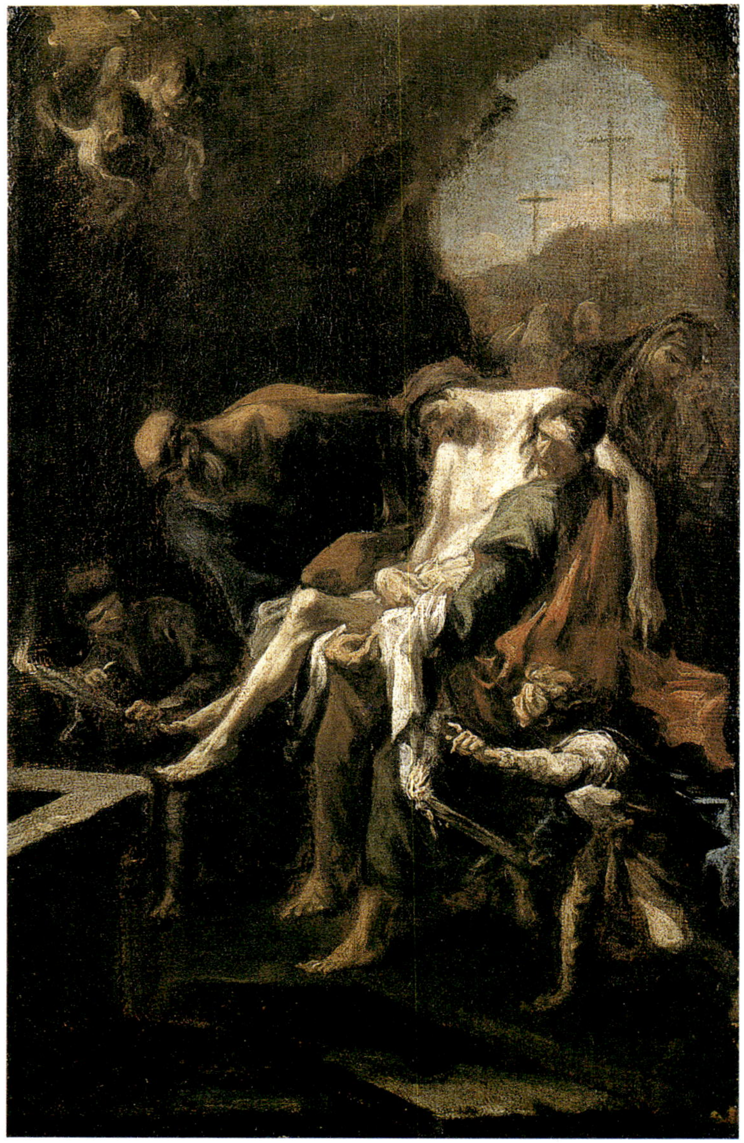

Works of art gather under an umbrella of words usually ending in 'ism'. To know all these terms is a luxury rather than a necessity when it comes to enjoying pictures. In the twentieth century, especially, many artists feel naked without an ism to hide behind and a new coinage seems to be minted every day. Usually these appear like shooting stars and disappear without a trace. Those that remain splinter into the usual derivatives and, if they repeat themselves, become neo-somethingism, to be succeeded in its turn by post-neo-somethingism until isms themselves seem in need of a collective noun (an obfuscation of isms perhaps).

Some of the most common forms of this kind of terminology are the most dangerous especially when used negatively or ideologically. Realism (p.46) is the most insidious denizen of the ismic underworld and keeps on popping up to accuse every new step taken in art of being a betrayal. Most official art thinks itself a version of Realism: those optimistic fictions behind whose sunny facades whole nations wilted and crumbled or ran with blood were called Socialist Realism. Naturalism is scarcely less dangerous and shares with Realism an ignorance of art's true possibilities (art can neither be realistic nor naturalistic).

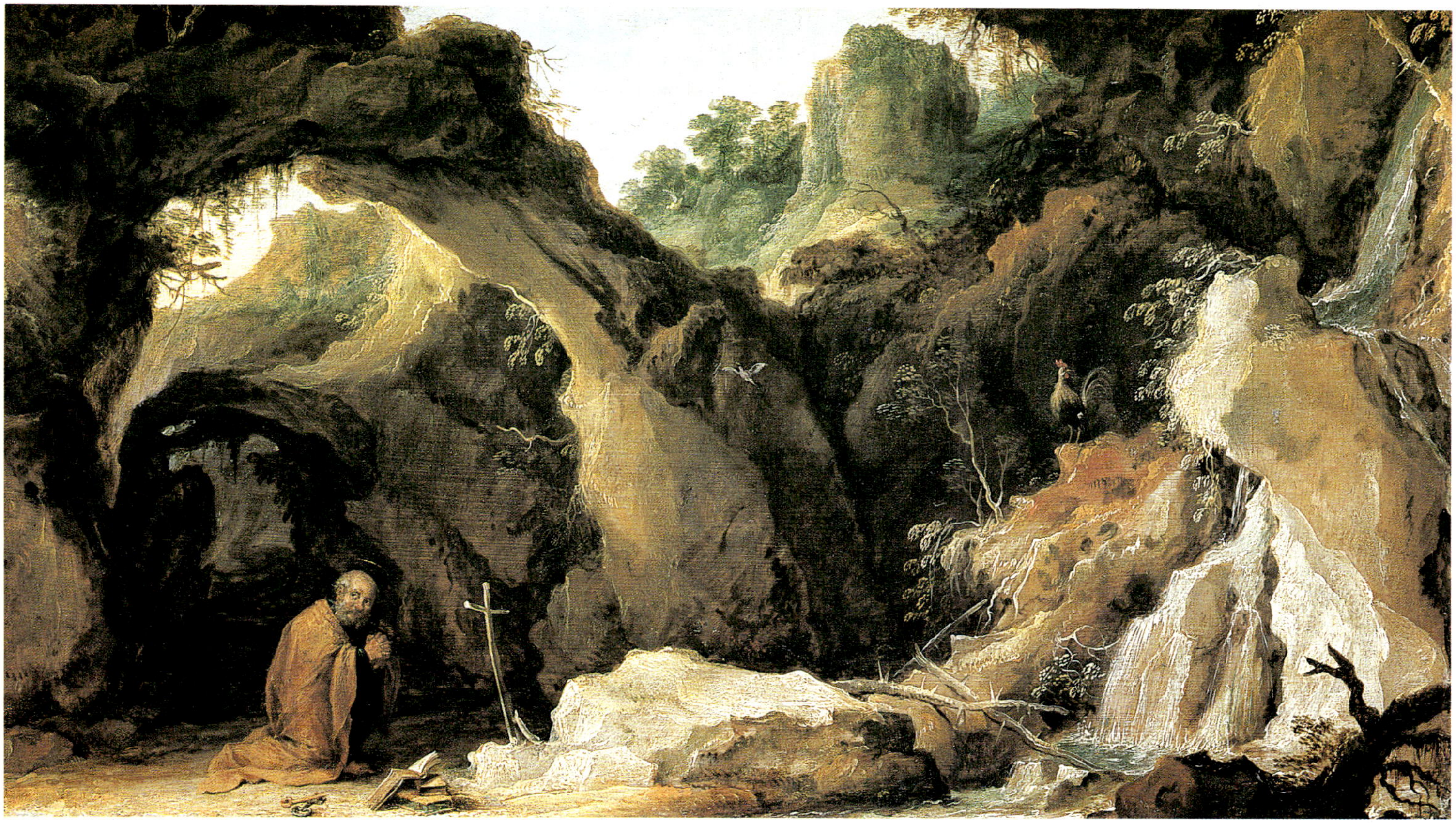

Too many of these labels are temptingly handy but they tend to narrow down the ways of looking at art. To take the common terms Classicism and Romanticism: if neo-classicism represents a revival of the classical past (with all its mythology and its conjectured aesthetic) then such a revival, being based on sentiment, is itself a *Romantic* phenomenon. Poussin's *Rinaldo and Armida* (p.63) could be a moment from a Romantic opera.[1]

As general stylistic markers isms are useful if handled roughly. Most of the pictures in the gallery are by painters innocent of isms in their own day. Some of them however look almost uncannily forward to movements in art yet to be born. In Magnasco's troubled and flickering world, where everyone is sick and usually emaciated and exists in an equally perturbed landscape, all the seeds of Expressionism await their flowering in Germany over two hundred years later. Similarly the grotesque forms and sinister disquiet of Surrealism can be seen in the sexually charged and hallucinatory landscape of the elder Teniers.[2] Both of these pictures would come under the art historian's heading of Mannerism, a nicely vague term which can include all eccentricities of vision or departures from mainstream styles.

Part of the trouble with this labelling fixation is that it makes art sound difficult and for experts only: it suggests that if you don't know rubrics such as Neo-Post-Painterly- Abstract-Expressionism you cannot follow what is going on in a picture. This is the equivalent of saying if you don't know a blackbird's ornithological name is *turdus merula* you cannot appreciate its song. The best rule to remember is that if you have enjoyed a painting you have understood it.

[1] No painter has been borrowed from more frequently by the producers of opera in terms of light, colour, atmosphere and grouping. Film directors owe him a thing or two as well.
[2] Expressionism (which is still alive and kicking) is characterised by *angst* and agitation in usual definitions. In one sense it is about not suppressing reactions; by painting with instinct, gestures of the brush are at one with the subject and the emotions it gives rise to. Surrealism has at its centre the release of the irrational world of dreams into the vocabulary of images.

J is for Journey

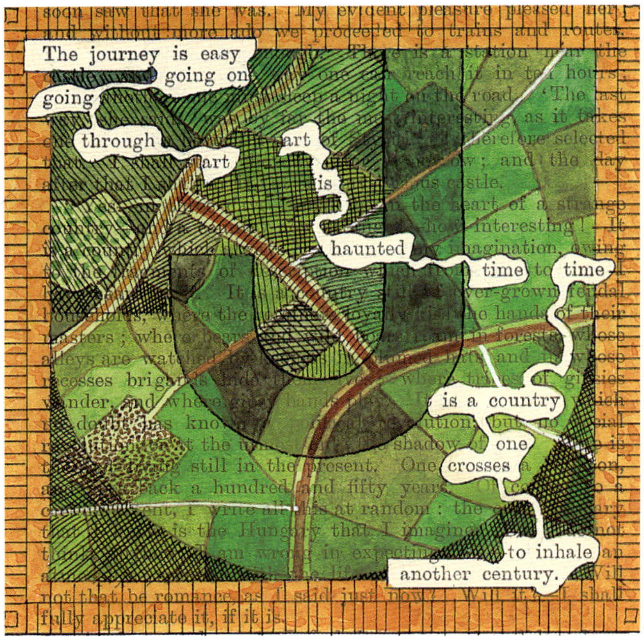

Unlike the sciences art gets no better. There is no destination of greater accuracy or universality to which it is travelling. We expect science to make progress: new science elbows out the old and fresh theories make their predecessors redundant. Art makes quite a different journey through time. Although discoveries are made and inventions constantly occur the paintings of the present do not in any sense make those of the past look mistaken or stupid. The journey began with paintings of the highest quality in caves thirty-thousand years ago and we can stop off at any point between then and now and find equally great masterpieces, be they in Lascaux, Pompeii, Renaissance Florence, Paris, or New York in our own century; not to mention wonders from other continents.

Of course it is also true of science that the *quality* of great mathematics or physics does not really change. Pythagoras, Galileo and Newton were the equals of Einstein and his successors. Yet their artistic equivalents are very much alive for us: nothing has replaced Giotto or Rembrandt and nothing will depose Picasso and Matisse. Art just gets richer; work in its store never loses its relevance. There are it is true some kinds of linear advancement; Cezanne is not possible without Poussin nor Picasso without Cezanne but, in contrast to the ever forward-pointing march of science, Cezanne's pictures serve to deepen our enjoyment of Poussin.

The Dulwich Picture Gallery is part of the receding past yet it constantly changes while acquiring no new pictures. Its best paintings get better as we see them in the light not only of a lengthening history of art but of more recent developments in thought. [1] Some of the works will reveal themselves as 'sleepers' whose moment of fashion or rediscovery has yet to come.

Walking through such a collection (which itself includes so many pictures of journeys; peasants with their loads, toffs out for a ride, or the great travellers of mythology) one sees, as well as the broad highways of portraiture and narrative painting, those many diversions that art makes into previously neglected areas. The sudden interest in flower painting in the Netherlands subsides within a hundred years (p.32/33) as does the boom in souvenir views of Italy (and Venice in particular). (p.16/17) One of the most curious of these diversions is the taste for slumming. Patrons of art liked to look upon the best and worst of times and were as fascinated by the hovels and haunts of the peasantry as they were by the banquets and extravagances of the court.

This tavern scene looks like the bottom of life's barrel. If one could hear its soundtrack it would be a raucous affair: drunken song and grating laughter would commingle with scrawny music and the noise of abused anatomies; farting, belching or grunting in hurried copulation, accompanied by the trickling sound of the semi-conscious stand-up tragedian urinating against the pillar. Although these peasants smoke [2] and drink their lives away when briefly freed from toil they are strangely redeemed by Brouwer's beautiful touch. No vase of flowers or view in the evening sun is graced with a more sensitive and subtle brush and this gives the picture its fascinating tension. Art never quite returns to such a spot again after this period in the Low Countries. If it revisits taverns it is to meet a more idealised rustic in a Pickwickian inn or the romantic inhabitants of *la vie de Bohème* in their more decorous squalor.

---

[1] We see more in Gainsborough now through the discoveries of Monet and Renoir etc. We feed modern psychological ideas, literary concepts and aesthetic theories into works that knew nothing of these things except by intuition.

[2] It is not tobacco they are smoking but an illegal mixture of belladonna and hemp.

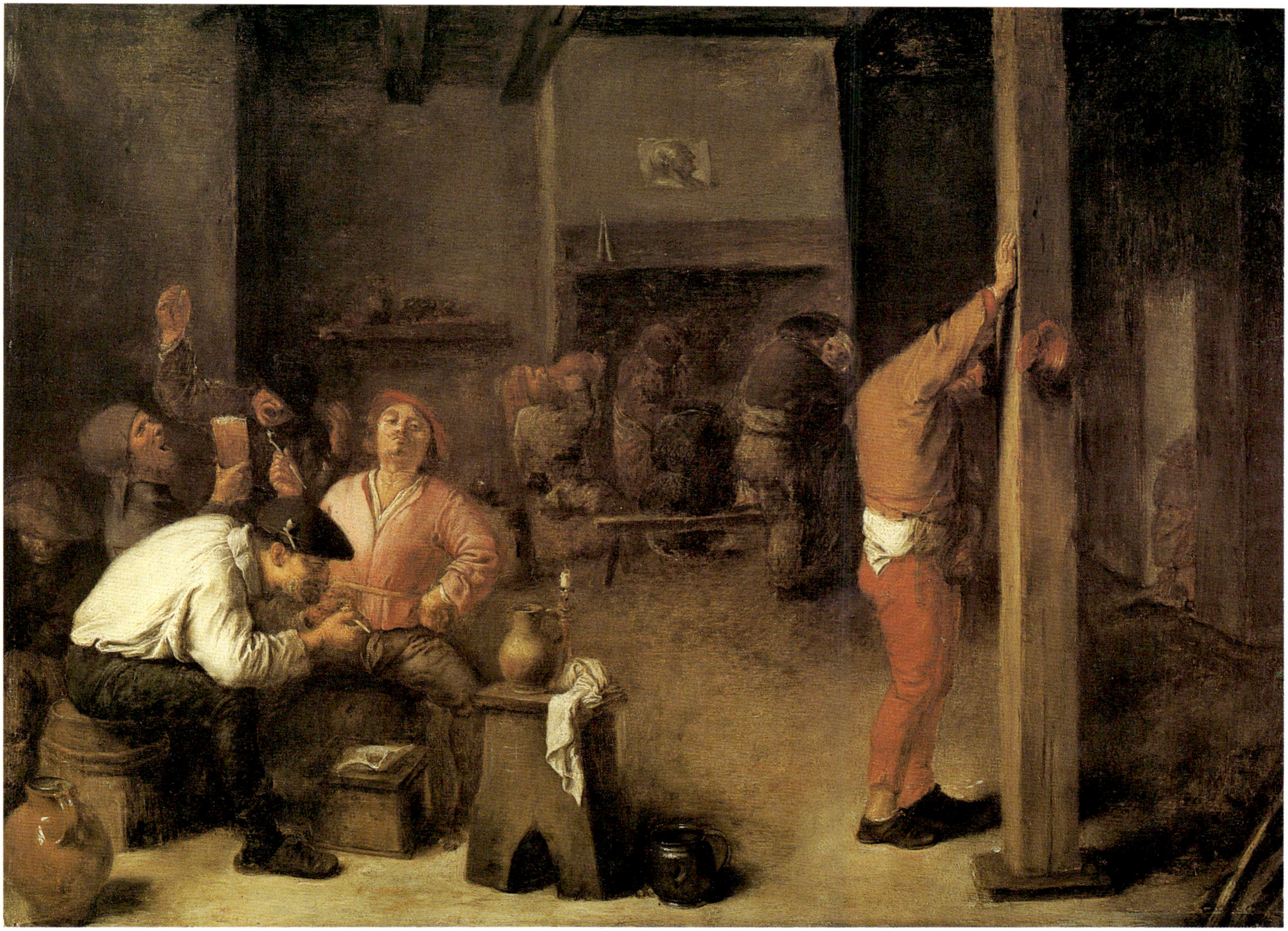

K is for Kitchen

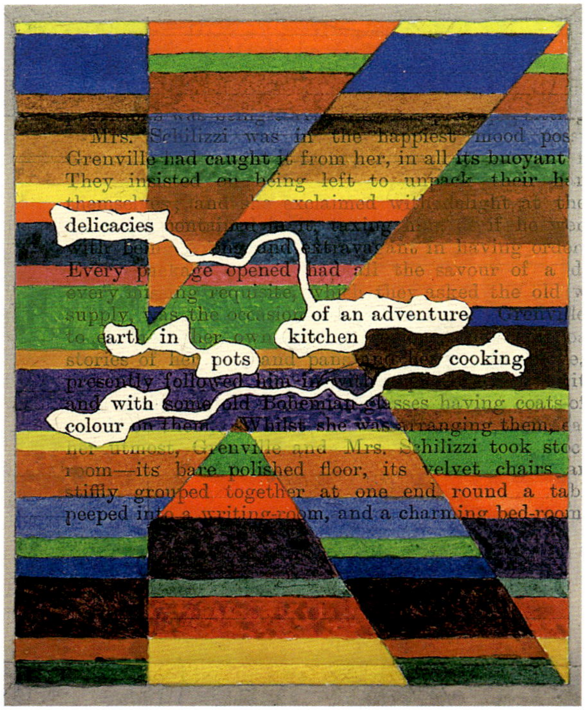

Life is raw and art is cooked. The writer crouches over his simmering word processor, the composer measures out and combines the mixtures of harmony and the spices of orchestration, but the most physical and kitcheny place of all is the artist's studio with its implements and endless rituals of preparation. Like good cooks, the artists of the past presented their dishes with all the effort of their making concealed.

Some studios were like the kitchens of great restaurants whose tasks are shared amongst many helpers with various degrees of responsibility, from bottle-washer to head chef. A leading artist's studio had its parallel levels of assistants, sometimes more than a dozen.

The picture opposite was made in a studio of a more modest kind [1] where fewer works would be on the go at any one time, yet van Huysum's workshop was doubly a kitchen in that the pictures had ingredients as well as the materials used on the canvases themselves.

Van Huysum probably only used one or two rather menial helpers, [2] but the labour of grinding colours from the blocks of mineral and preparing surfaces for mixing, would have taken all their time, in an age before paint came in labelled tubes and oils arrived ready-mixed in bottles. The other ingredients necessary for his work would have come from the flower and vegetable market. Both paints and blooms could be expensive. [3]

Most people would call the flower painting opposite 'naturalistic' but no form of art involved more artifice, trickery and devices than the classical Dutch flower painting. Everything is a fiction, nothing you see is actually happening. The composition is as contrived as that of the Veronese altarpiece must have been (p.14) and is based on a similar descent of lights and darks. Even the general situation of luminous floral abundance in a black world is a contradiction in practical terms. The flowers themselves defy the seasons as much as today's freezer-reliant cookery: they would not have been in bloom at the same time of year or even, in van Huysum's case (for he was prone to giving the dates of his pictures as covering a two year period), in the same year at all. Bloom would be patiently added to bloom and that year's beetle would feed on last year's leaf. In order to praise nature (and it was a highly artificial and cultivated nature) nature was expunged. The bird's nest, a signature device, appears with small variations in most of his pictures and is taken from stock.

But as with a kitchen, the ingredients do not make the dish. All depends on the cook. The feebler artists of the time had at their disposal the same pigments and paraphernalia, the same flowers and vegetation as did van Huysum, who made from them such hypnotic masterpieces.

---

[1] Van Huysum was one of the most successful artists in history. His paintings are now priced in millions and were not far off the equivalent value when they were painted.

[2] Not only does he seem to have been a grumpy individual (not all nice pictures are painted by nice people) but his paranoia made him avoid having pupils bright enough to steal his secrets.

[3] Although by this time the great wave of tulipomania (when tulips were as valuable as houses) had passed, the most expensive flowers were still pricier than paintings of them by competent masters.

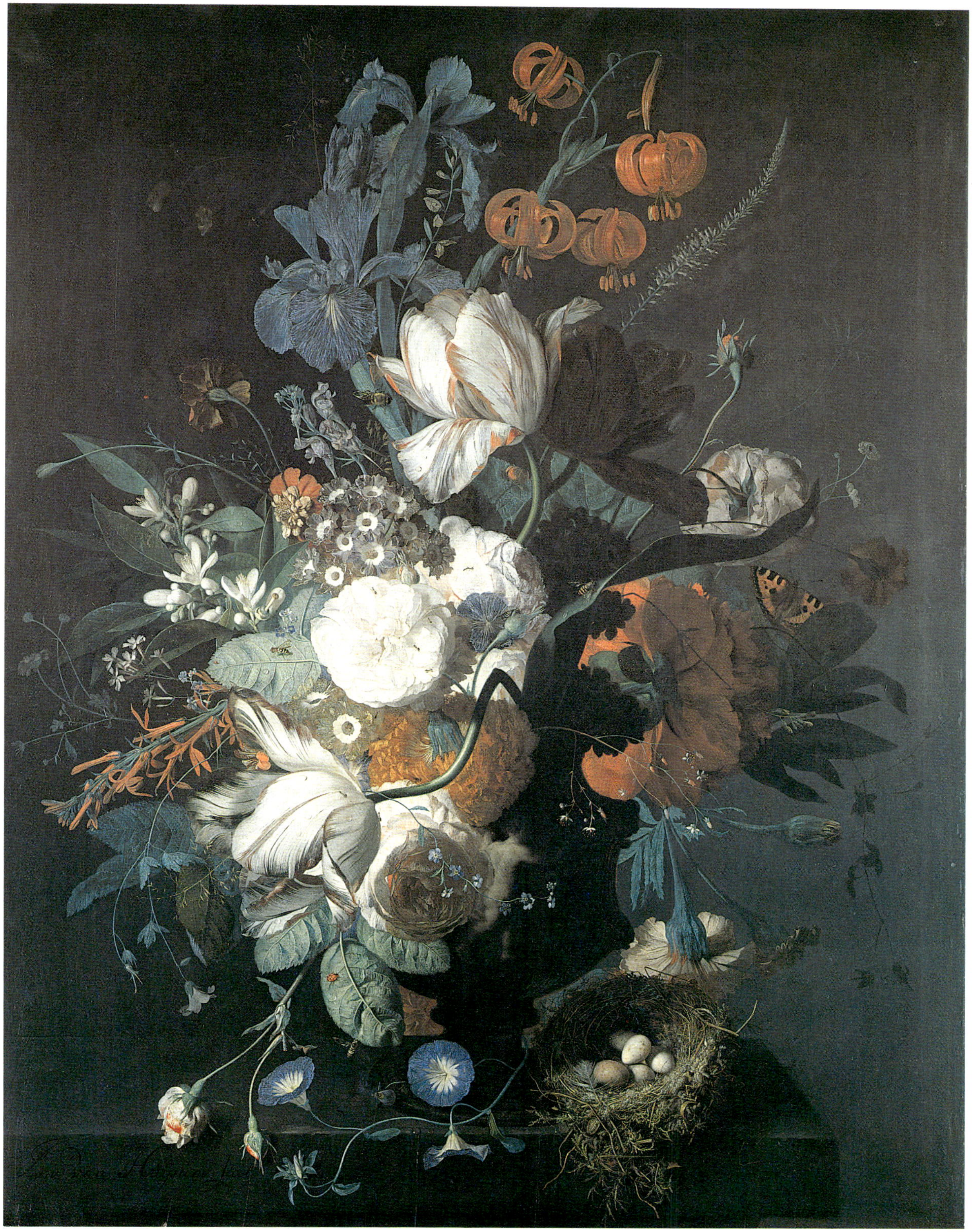

L is for Landscape

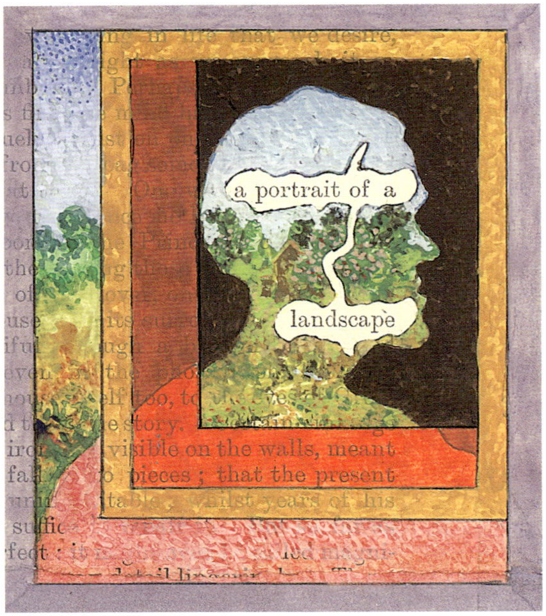

Landscape is an invention of art. Nature has always been around but landscape is a version of nature tamed, defined, and even framed, by art. It is no accident that we call an admired view 'picturesque'. For centuries the painter has been making fragments of nature coherent and acceptable so that they can be manageably seen. Each of us as a result now has a mental framing device [1] that we can hold up to the unbounded chaos of our random perception of the world around us. Every generation of artists (the process still goes on) returns from the wild with a new bit of nature to add to the inventory of 'the beautiful'.

Eventually the landscape itself, as (in England especially) a conspiracy between God and the farmer or landowner, starts to behave like a painting. The landed gentry would arrange their acres in collusion with art by a process significantly called landscape-gardening. Often, paradoxically, the wildness of a view was itself cultivated; hills moved to better positions, waterfalls and grottoes engineered and even picturesque people (hermits to inhabit the custom-built cave) imported. This process came full circle when an artist was commissioned to paint the 'artistic' result.

In the landscape of Tivoli opposite, the artist is telling the truth in the form of a lie. He paints himself painting a view; an obvious impossibility. What he has done, of course, is to paint a view and put himself in it painting another view he has probably never painted. The picture we see here was undoubtedly cooked in the studio from ingredients gathered at the spot in the form of sketches and notes. The moment of golden light that he depicts is only transitory and in any case the action of painting a picture over a metre in length out of doors is a perilous business.[2] In the studio he can rearrange nature to taste, with the necessary elements of foreground interest, with people in the middle-distance, to add scale and a series of controlled receding planes.

What Richard Wilson [3] is also saying for the benefit of his English clientele is, 'I am here in Italy, the home of painting, and I bring back stylistic news as well as this famous view'. By including himself he seems to be his own corroborative witness. The landscape also incorporates, as a final flattery to its future owner, a view of what is taken to be the villa of Maecenas, the greatest art patron of Augustan Rome.

This mellow and elegant landscape is perhaps the final tweak in the paradox of nature imitating art. The painter himself has become part of the picturesque, joining nymph, shepherd and salaried hermit as one of the cast of pastoral mythology.

[1] This now, of course, takes a mechanical form as in the viewfinder (note the term) of a camera.

[2] In the painting he is shown working with his canvas set up against the light which would make painting a difficult affair. Furthermore, canvas is the same material as sail cloth (ship's chandlers were its original suppliers) and can easily take off in the wind.

[3] Richard Wilson was a founder-member of the Royal Academy in the eighteenth century. He started his career as a portrait painter but found greater success as a landscapist. The text in the initial appropriately echoes HWK Collam's *Come Autumn Hand*:

> Behind is the landscape, portrait of a place:
> before it the likeness, landscape of a face.

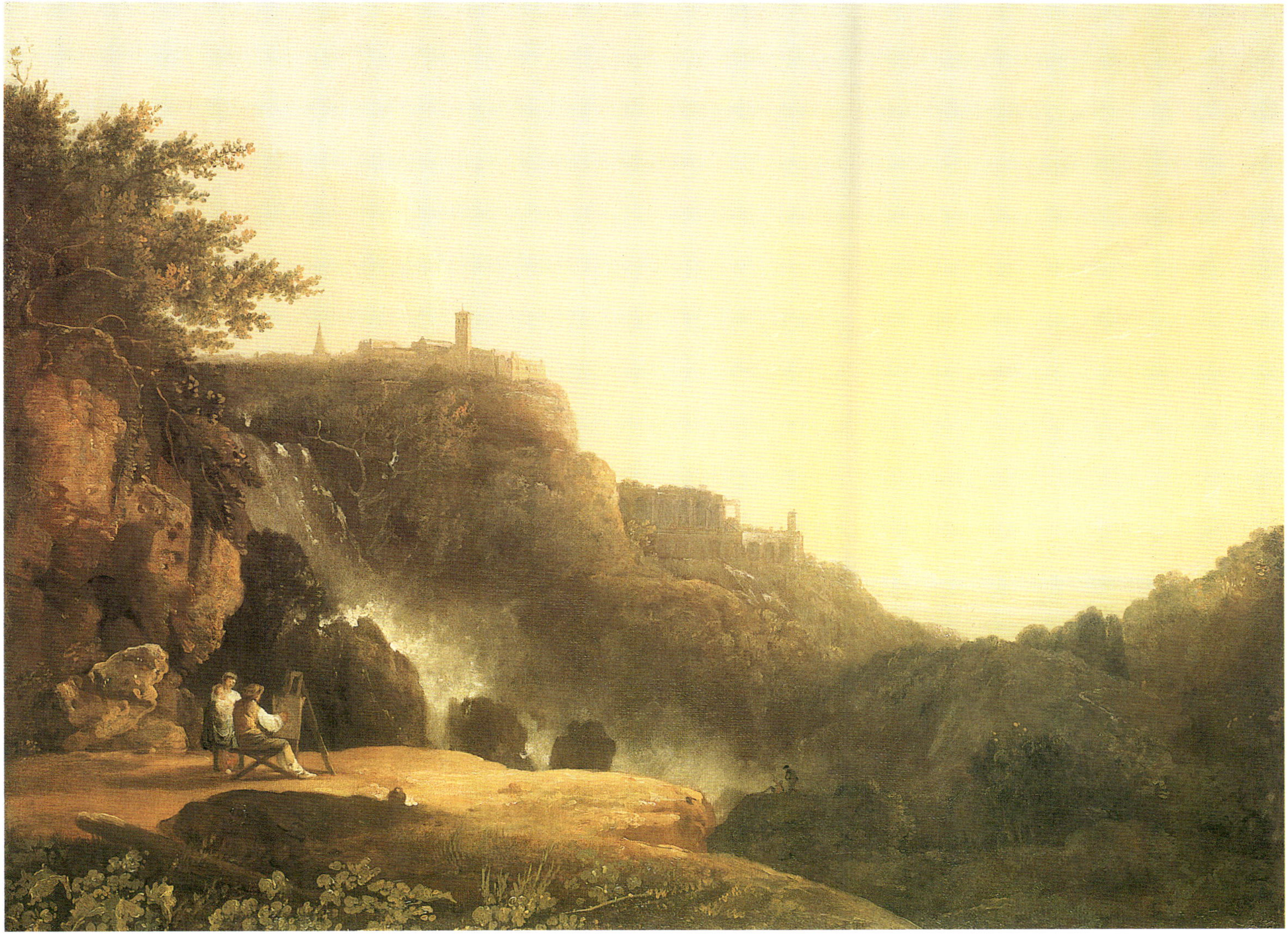

M is for Mythology

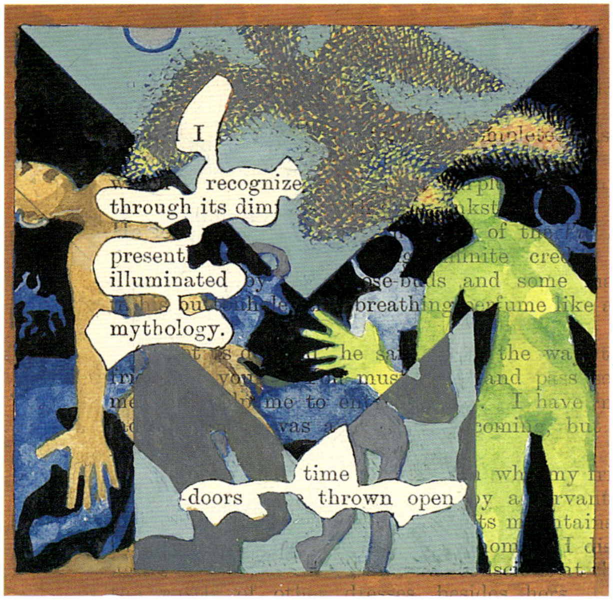

Outside the areas of portraiture, landscape and still-life, all painting is about mythology. Even a landscape can have mythic overtones or be dimly peopled by strange gods, and, in the wider sense of making an ikon, the portrait itself can create mythical status.[1] Mythology is ceaselessly manufactured and in each century there are fictions which act as such strong identifiers of the human condition that their tales become known to millions who have no idea of their source. Few have read *Frankenstein*, but his monster is a universal point of reference, more so than its Jewish equivalent, the Golem.

It is we that have the archetypes (perhaps literally) in our brains and wait for myths to match them. The spaces are vacant or inappropriately occupied until Samson or Cinderella comes along.

Painting is here a poor relation since unlike literature it seems unable to make myths out of thin air: children's tales do it better. Its employment is found in the corroboration trade and sometimes at the shabby end. It gives form and shape to what is told. It is difficult to shake free from the mental pictures that art has given us. For instance, in christian mythology, nowhere does the Bible speak of a thin pale man with a beard, yet the wall of my Sunday School was hung with anaemic derivatives of the Jesus of Raphael: no one even mentioned the possibility of his being a strongly-built, swarthy, clean shaven, middle-eastern Jew.

For many centuries, with the church as chief patron, painting had to toe the party line. The intellectual emancipation of the Renaissance opened up that second great storehouse of mythological subjects, classical literature. The engines of both the Bible and the texts of the Ancient World pointed to Rome with its empire as the ends of their respective journeys. This made possible a generic never-never land devised by artists where scenes from either mythology could take place in the appropriate timeless clothing.

Thus we do not find it absurd that David returns with the head of Goliath [2] along a street lined with classical arches and pillars to be welcomed by a suspiciously Greco-Roman looking crowd. In this way painting did succeed if not in the making of myths then in the construction of a visual universe where mythological scenes could be enacted; the space that would stand for 'the olden days', and could last to Hollywood and beyond. All the efforts of the archeologists of biblical lands (and their diligently authentic tableaux or dioramas in the museums of the world) cannot beat Raphael, Poussin and Cecil B. de Mille.

Once biblical and classical forces had made some sort of truce no rival system stood a chance. The teutonic gods and northern legends [3] were banished like Ignorance from Tiepolo's allegory, defeated by Fame. Giambattista Tiepolo was the great virtuoso painter of the eighteenth century, who could deal even-handedly with all mythological orthodoxies and add, as in this case, a kind of civic allegory to the mixture.

The team that would execute the ceiling from this sketch (done by Giambattista in a few hours) was essentially a family firm. They seemed to have acted as models as well as painters and technicians, for almost everyone in their paintings has the same cast of features. We know from correspondence that the actual ceiling would take, including the interruptions Tiepolo complained of, not much more than a month. The iconography of heaven and Olympus is present in this unspecified incident whose symbolic figures are variously identified but whose gist is clear (the forces of light defeat the forces of darkness and are glorified). No one can throw gods or virtues or saints up on a ceiling like Tiepolo and make them seem such natural inhabitants of instantly limpid skies.

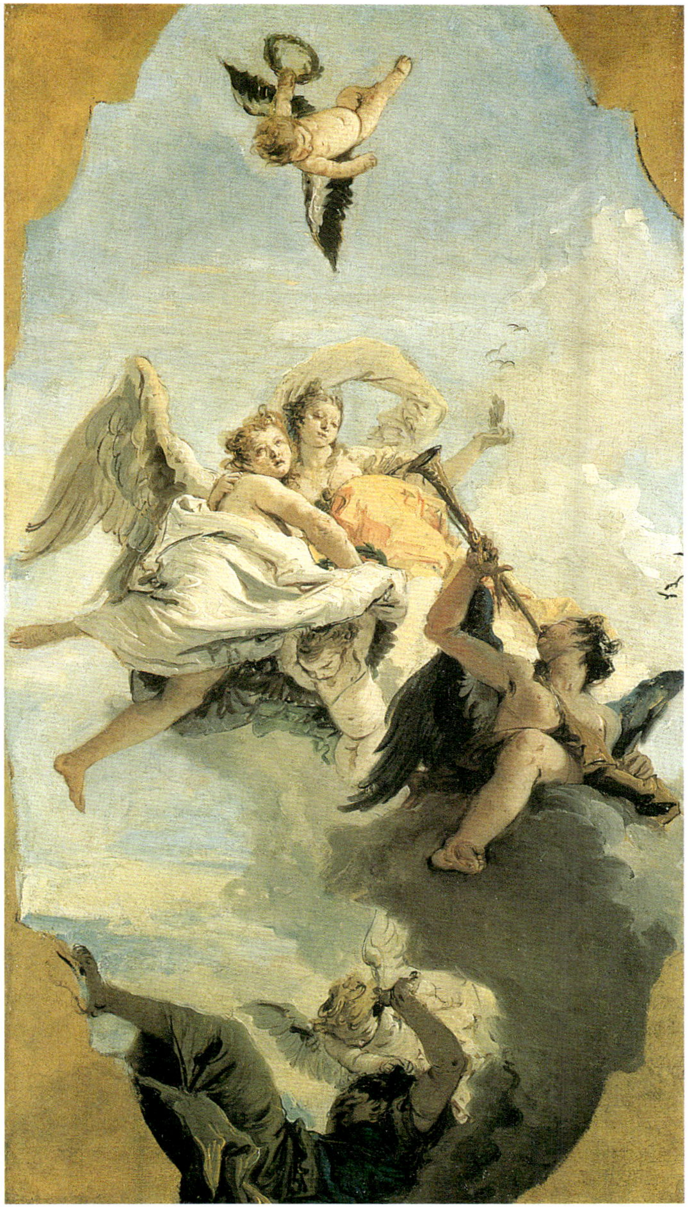

The final triumph of painting's service to mythology is to have made cities, fields and aerial habitats which, once the gods have departed and saints and angels have moved off, can be settled happily by Temperance, Motherhood, Agriculture and the Dance, or rented out to Empire, Monarchy, Music and all their friends.

[1] One thinks of Holbein's Henry VIII as a propagandist ikon to make a myth of kingship.

[2] Poussin makes Goliath real by creating a head of a plausible giant with circumstantial measurement. If David is my (average) height, then Goliath, comparing head measurements, must be a reasonable four metres high or just under.

[3] Wagner of course in the *Ring of the Nibelung* went against the grain and used precisely these gods and stories. Since they were, by the end of the nineteenth century, little known, he could take all sorts of liberties which he would not have had license for in the classical pantheon.

N is for Naked/Nude

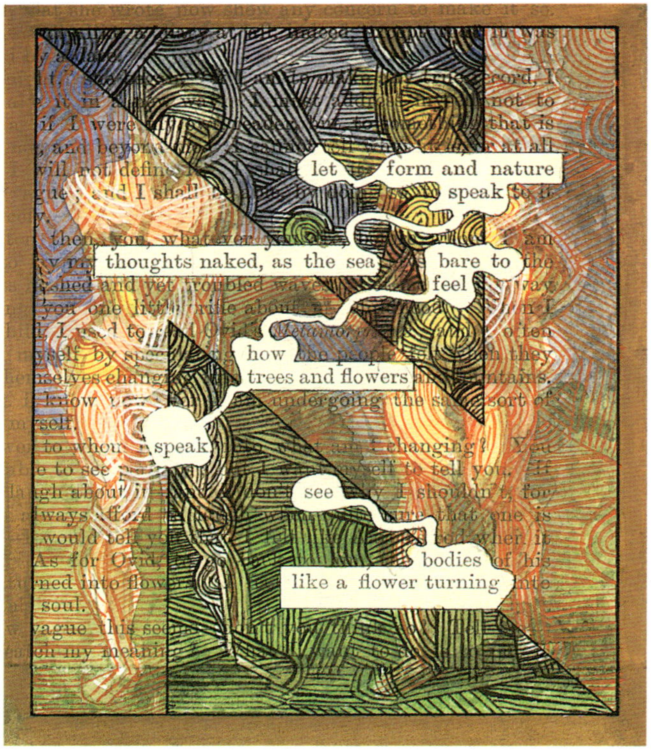

When does the naked become the nude? All nudes are of course naked, but at what point does the promotion from one definition to another take place? Were the first nudes also the last? Adam and Eve were presumably nude until the eating of the apple from the Tree of Knowledge told them they were naked.[1] In every-day usage the two words shift uneasily from foot to foot. Sex shops feature nudes but this may indicate artistic pretensions, like those tableaux of quivering flesh that were a feature of the declining music-hall.[2]

The picture opposite gives a clue. All the figures except one seem to me to be naked. The erotically recumbent body, made more suggestive by the shade which enfolds her and the drapery, rocks and foliage which are about to embrace her, is a nude with a pedigree in art since she is in a characteristic pose of seductive promise. The others are a very mixed bunch. Art is an alchemy and it was obviously the intention that these figures would magically represent the great pastoral dream while retaining their substance as sexual beings.

Somehow everything has gone wrong: instead of being transported to a glade in Arcadia we remain in the artist's studio aware of cloths piled up on cushions to prop up the poses. These women know their nakedness and are being paid for it by the hour. The gentle slumber of nymphs looks too much like the exhausted sleep of working women. It is difficult to tell how many were involved: the two foreground figures are possibly views of the same model who in fact may have served for all the assembled cast. In terms of the space created in the picture there simply is not enough room for all these bodies. The hunched figure at the back of the group looks like an afterthought: the artist seems not to have been able to make a plausible foot for his erotic nude, and has had to cover it up in desperation with yet another drowsy Arcadian.

For all that the three principal figures are expertly painted, the life-studies made in the studio, squared up and transferred to canvas, have not metamorphosed into sylvan divinities.

In the right hand corner the standard group of *putti* (as these baroque babies are called) makes quite a performance with a dolphin to form a sculpted fountain which nevertheless only produces the merest trickle of water.

One almost wonders if Lely[3] is playing a sophisticated game via this sculpture and the resting wood-spirits, and is actually discussing, in paint, the problem of the naked and the nude. Until, that is, one looks again at that fudged foot and the unconvincing half-head that so clumsily masks it. The fountain seems in the end to be a metaphor for a grand labour producing diminished returns.

---

[1] The primal couple of Old Testament mythology are quoted in the initial letter, which derives from the gallery's painting by a follower of Mabuse. It is presumably to recapture this lost state of unembarrassed acceptance of the body that the cult of nudism (also, significantly, called naturism) exists. Topless bathers, streakers etc. tend to emphasize rather than challenge the taboo.

[2] Female nudity was permitted on stage as long as the bodies did not move: wobbling did not seem to count as movement, judging by the last of such shows that I saw at the Empress Brixton, which was sadly titled: *We couldn't wear less.*

[3] Peter Lely, who was made Sir Peter just before he died at the age of 62, was described by Pepys as 'a mighty proud man and full of state'. He became a master painter in his native Holland when he was nineteen. He built up a hugely successful practice as a portrait painter, in England, a livelihood that has always (in exchange for a certain drudgery) provided rich pickings.

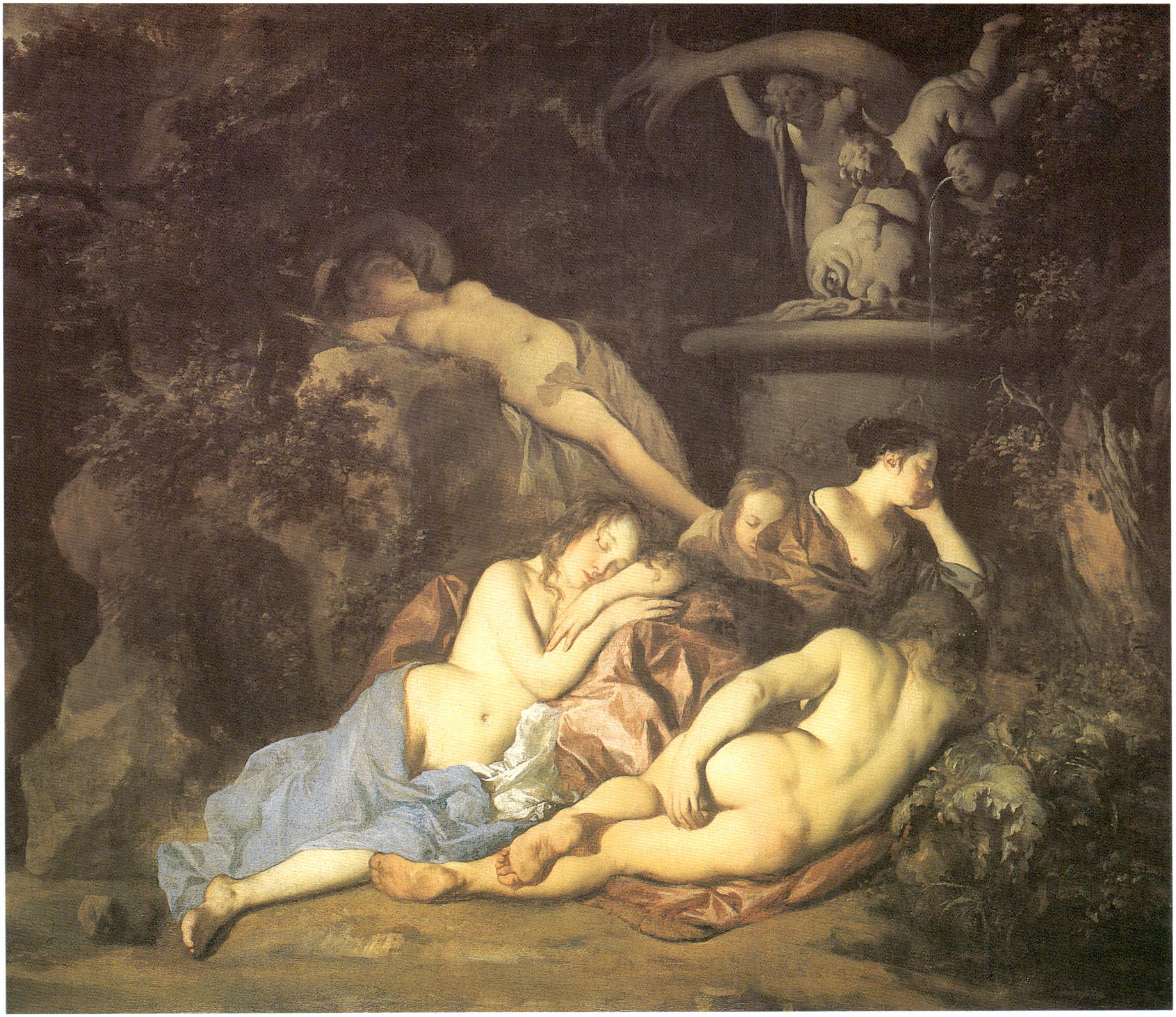

O is for Ornament

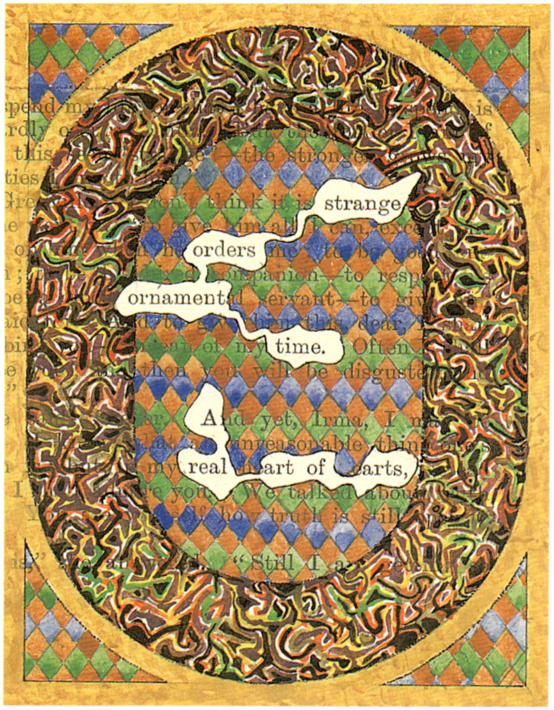

Ornament is where abstract art has had its hiding place for thousands of years. It is often made of elements which form a pattern by their repetition. Almost any configuration of straight lines or curves, rhythmically repeated, acquires a certain magic as every doodler knows (doodling itself being the last innocent alibi for many self-styled inartistic adults). Ancient civilizations knew this well and the first traces of mankind's aesthetic aspirations appear as ornament on bone, shell and rock-face over forty thousand years ago. [1] Once pottery was in production pattern became a language by which the archeologist is able now read the shifts of ancient cultures.

Thus ornament lies at the heart of the matter in art and provides one of the two great threads (figuration and abstraction) that run throughout its history, coexisting, joining, overlapping and separating. Those very spirals and linear patterns of circle, zigzag, loop and chevron which appear on prehistoric rocks are still part of the grammar of picture making (p.22/23).

Although they can seem playfully abstract, ornamental devices often obey stricter natural laws than many kinds of representation: they have their starting point in the principles of plant growth (the unfurling of ferns etc.) or in fish scales, or the hidden mathematics of the play of wind on sand or sea. They are usually based on the keenest observation.

Even in the glummest portrait there are usually moments of ornamental relief; a fancy collar or a patterned shawl. Although the arts have sometimes become separated despite their unified beginnings at the dawn of prehistory, they frequently link up through quotation in this way.

Except for the red tablecloth and the general all-purpose portrait gloom in which this grandee stands, everything in this painting is either ornamental or ornamented. The combination of armour and lace, although normal enough in an aristocratic seventeenth-century portrait, now seems a confusion of messages. Evidently the highly-worked and decorative ruff would have to be removed (an easy task since it could be collapsed like a christmas decoration into a starched concertina) in order to put on the elaborate helmet with its high plumes. The cuffs would in their turn, be surrendered to the gauntlets.

Armour was at the period an item that declared your wealth and taste. Such an outfit as this, magnificently chased with an intricate heraldic pattern, is more than done justice to by van Dyck: the picture was after all a speculative showpiece to establish himself as a portrait painter on his arrival in Sicily. Hence the ornament is fully rendered rather than suggested.

The twenty-five year old painter shows off his technique and the thirty-six year old Prince shows off his metal finery, perhaps itself recently commissioned. [2] The armourer who so skillfully worked the repeating devices on breastplate and helmet, would have been considered the equal in craftsmanship to the young and eager artist we think of as so much more exalted. It is this divergence of status over time that has caused so many that should be celebrating our lives with fine design to crowd the more risky but glamorous profession of artist.

---

[1] Necklaces were found in Southern Africa, among forty-thousand-year-old deposits, made of ostrich eggshell beads, bitten first into rough discs and then refined into perfect circles by grinding on stone, a technique continuously in use from then till now.

[2] In which case both portrait and armour are sad ironies, for the Prince was not to outlive his likeness by more than a few weeks and van Dyck fled plague-ridden Palermo without painting another picture.

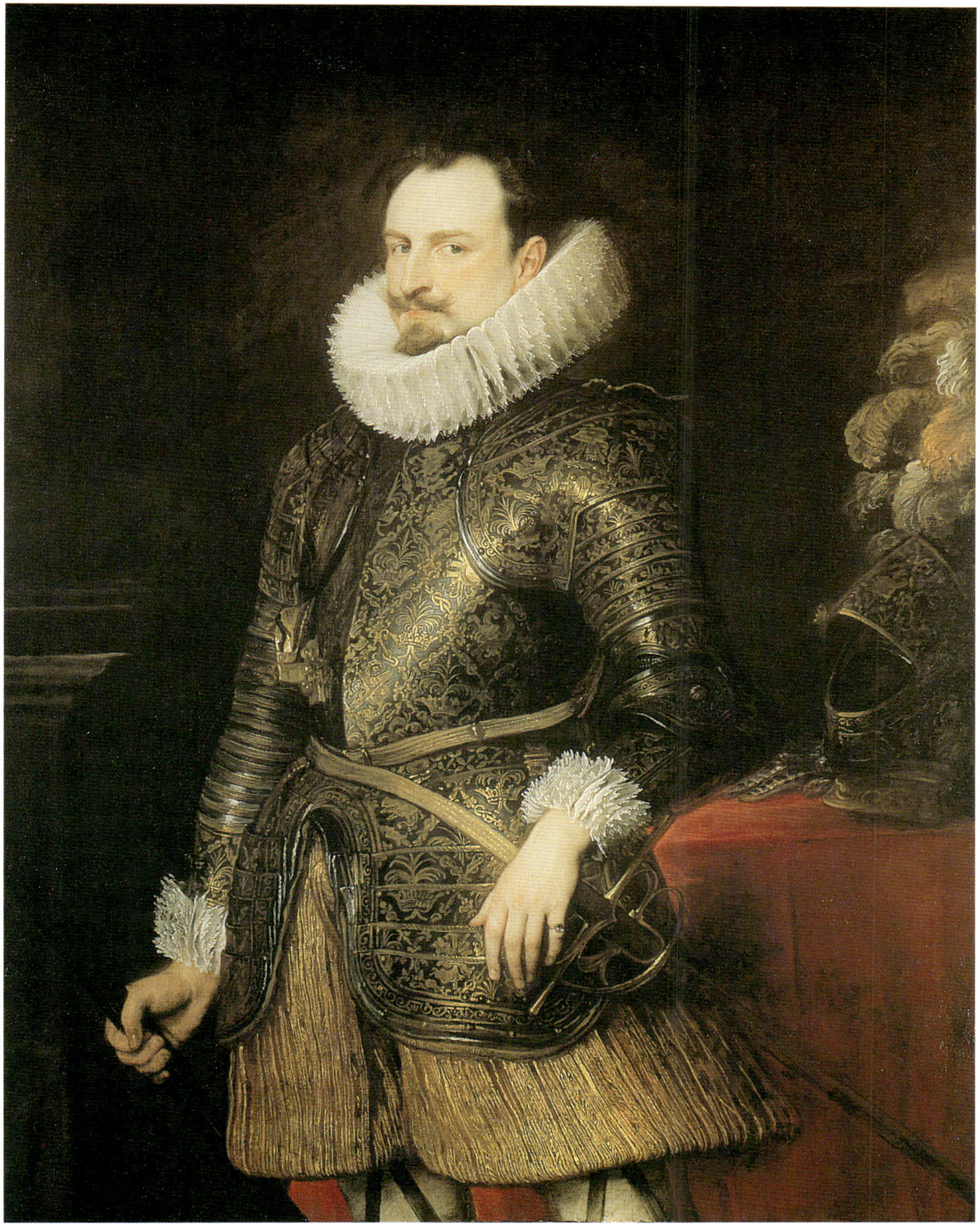

P is for Photograph

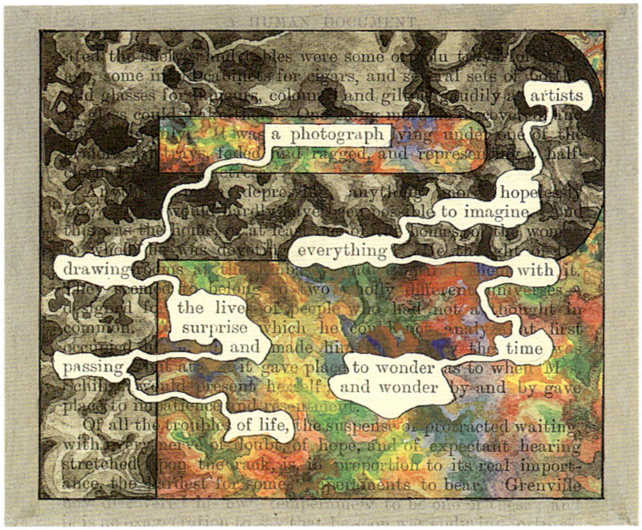

All the pictures in this book are mechanical reproductions via photography and therefore betray in their various ways the paintings they stand for (altering the balance of colour, ironing out the texture, reducing the scale etc.). Even so they can hardly ever, even at a glance, be mistaken for actual photographs of the people, objects and scenes they depict. Their origin as paintings asserts itself immediately. No sisters photographed in a garden are going to look like the Linley sisters (p.47), nor any encounter in a landscape resemble the meeting of Rinaldo and Armida[1] (p.63).

Photography was meant to put an end to painting, making it redundant as a way of talking about the world. This thought followed on from the fallacy that the goal of painting was some kind of rendered copy of 'reality' (p.46). The first great favour done to painting by photography was to release it from that false ambition, since of course it was soon realised that photographs themselves were not 'realistic'. The second favour was to liberate painting from some pretty boring chores. The jobbing portrait painter who trudged from village to village quickly invested in a camera; for all along he had been a photographer. Nonetheless portraiture survived and still thrives, for there is an essential difference in the business of painting a human likeness that the existence of photography makes more apparent. The painter's version of a face is made over a long period, (even the quickest sketch will take several thousand times longer than the average photograph) during which time many moods pass through the sitter's expression: the artist's view is a conflation of these and, therefore comprehensive whereas the photograph is the freezing of a particular and (and as anyone who has opened a packet of snaps on the way back from the chemist will know) not necessarily characteristic muscular moment.

The visual muddle that characterises the typical family snapshot with its clashing colours and harsh flesh-tones shows how difficult the grammar of colour really is. We were all quite good photographers until colour came along. Not only were black and white and the infinitude of grays in between as much as people could handle, but they lent a kind of poetry to the banal: their sobriety unified an incoherent world. That is why most serious photographers still work in black and white.

When a painting is reproduced in monochrome one can see that an important weapon of the good artist is control of tonality and that colour is not doing all the work. Just as a great symphony

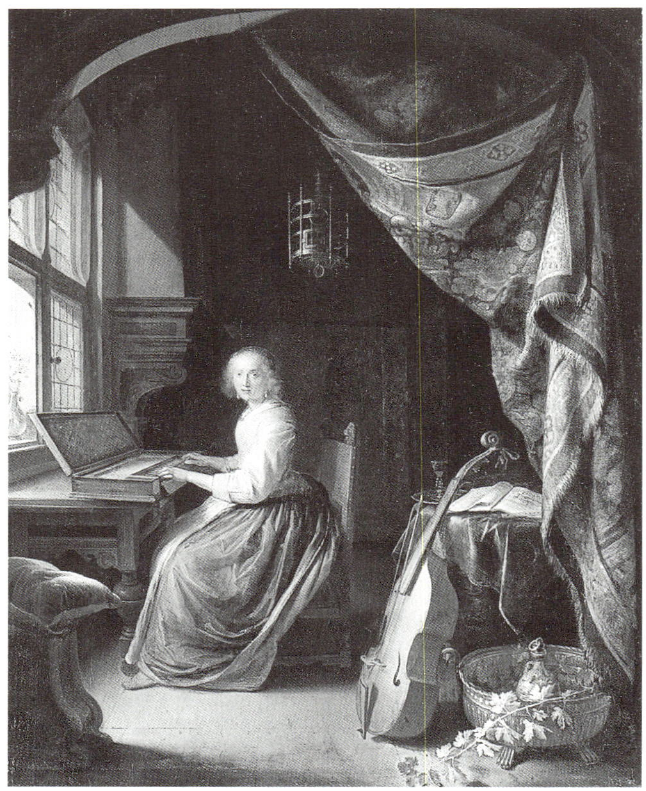

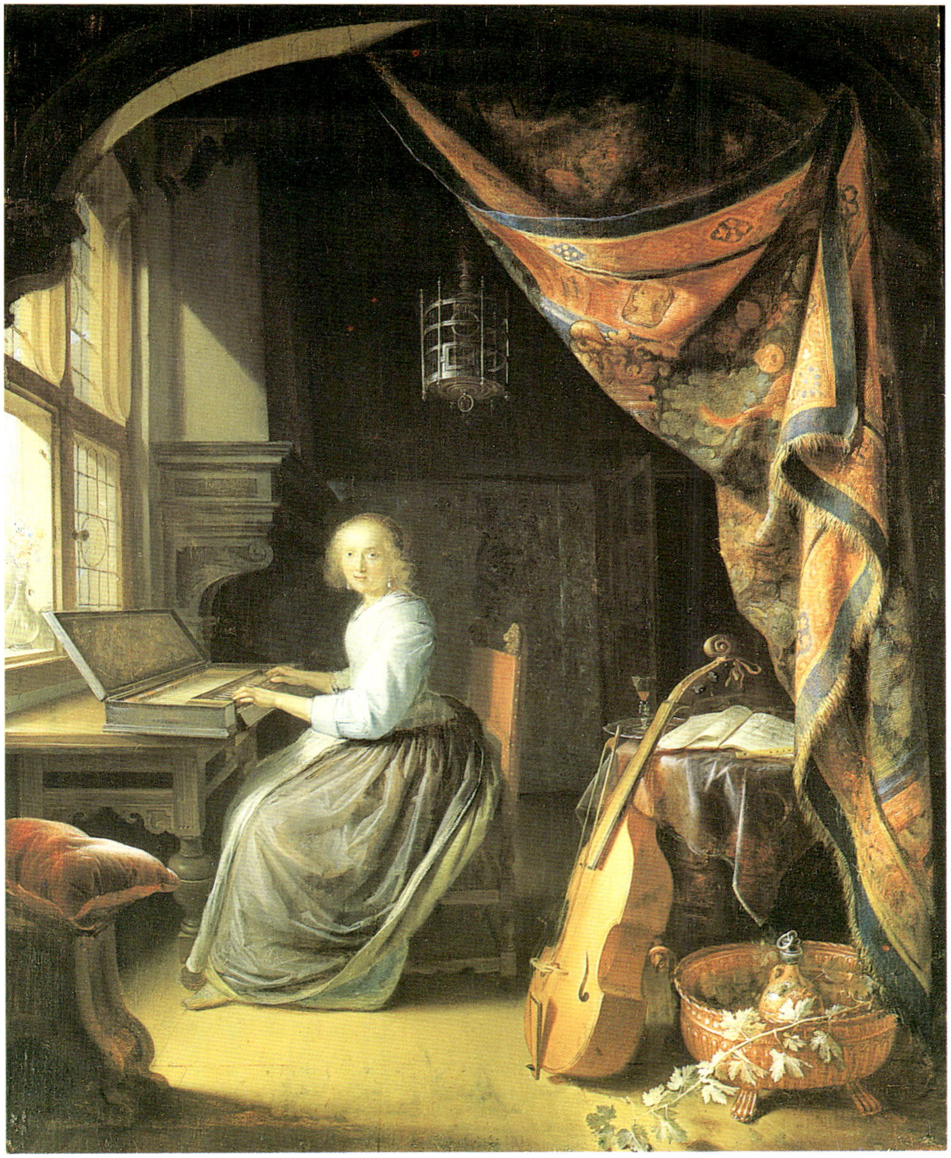

survives a piano transcription, so a high proportion of the virtues of a masterpiece can be seen in the absence of colour. Within a small area (less than 30cm. wide) Gerrit Dou [2] juggles his colour with virtually no recourse to black and white: he produces a basic harmony of warm hues with a restrained scattering of cool accents of blue and violet in the carpet, clothing and window. In monochrome, although the picture looks perfectly coherent, the light seems suddenly stagey and harsh, whereas in the original it is limpid and golden and settles gently where it lands.

To achieve this with a camera, the photographer would have to rearrange the world. The painter needs only to keep adjusting the picture within its closed repertoire of colour to realise his vision.

[1] And, needless to say, no parade is going to fall into the amazingly organised grouping with the arrangement of gestures, expressions etc. of Poussin's *Triumph of David.* (p.25)
[2] Gerrit Dou was a pupil of Rembrandt when Rembrandt himself was only in his twenties. It was Vermeer who later took up this subject and transmuted it into charmed miracles with similarly isolated females caught in liquid light.

Q is for Question

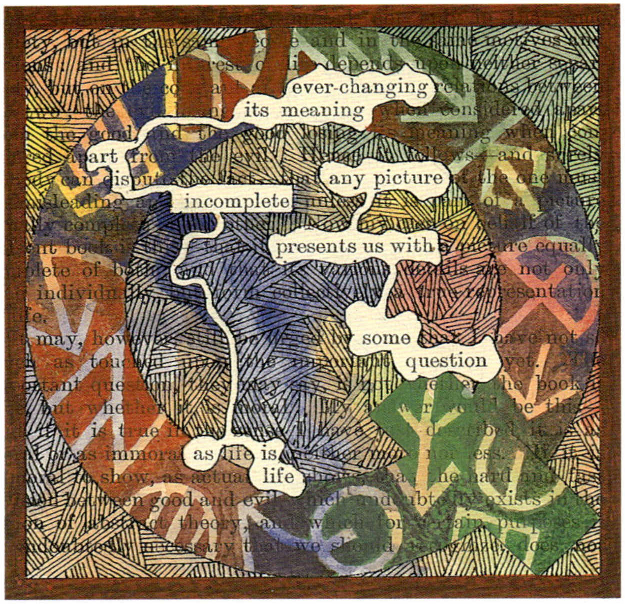

Every picture asks its own particular question, but the gallery as a whole asks a larger longer question: why have art at all? What is one doing in a building looking at representations of people and the world when just outside the door is the world itself plentifully peopled? Why look at pictures of flowers and trees when the gallery is virtually set in a park full of flowers and trees?

We seem to have a constant need for representations of ourselves and our situations and surroundings, not only from art but from plays, films, opera and photographs, cartoons and comedy. All these do what Shakespeare tells his actors they must do: they 'hold a mirror up to nature'. Through all these creative devices we stand as if in a fairground hall of mirrors, some flattering, some distorting. As well as reflecting us they reflect each other: the film echoes the theatre for example but also takes its sense of composing a flat image from painting. Painting, seeing its terms reflected in the cinema, returns the compliment. Even those who have never knowingly looked at painting have absorbed many of its inventions: the talking head on television has the portrait as its ancestor and obeys the same conventions.

We need art to make sense of the world. Any step beyond the hand to mouth and stone to break bone needs an aesthetic. Aesthetics, the study of the beautiful, would appear at first glance to be a minor backwater of philosophy: a subdivision of ethics; the study of what is right to do. Yet what is right to do must be judged by some formal idea, some overview of pattern which can only be called aesthetics; the measure of what is right in general. What is right to do is what it is beautiful to do and aesthetics can be viewed in one sense as the arbiter of human action and behaviour.

Mankind discovered this through art by making things better than they needed to be. Art dates back to the birth of uselessness, which is our liberation from mere survival. I recently had the privilege of curating an exhibition of the art of Africa,[1] that continent where the whole adventure of human life began. The initial exhibit was a stone axe from the Olduvai gorge in Tanzania, one and a half million years old, a roughly shaped tool, the first thing made by man. The second exhibit was from South Africa, another axe but made three-quarters of a million years later. This was suddenly an object of elegant proportions and brilliant craftsmanship. Its large scale put it already in the realm of the ceremonial or prestige object and its non-functional edges were as carefully engineered as any other part. Art had entered the human arena and was determining the need for quality in object and life: we can call this mystery the aesthetic imperative.

This universal desire for art is not only rooted deep in time, but also widely dispersed in space, for there is no culture or community that lacks a mode of expression that we would call art.[2] That the call for a language of artistic communication was of primal urgency is indicated by the presence of a comprehensive vocabulary of mark and sign which still forms the basis of drawing.

Wherever we find the remains of human communities we see how deep was the need for a visual language. All the elements that continue to form the basis of drawing today were in coherent use twenty-thousand years before the development of writing. Art is not a recent luxury but an old necessity.

It is not easy to explain why, when searching for a picture that

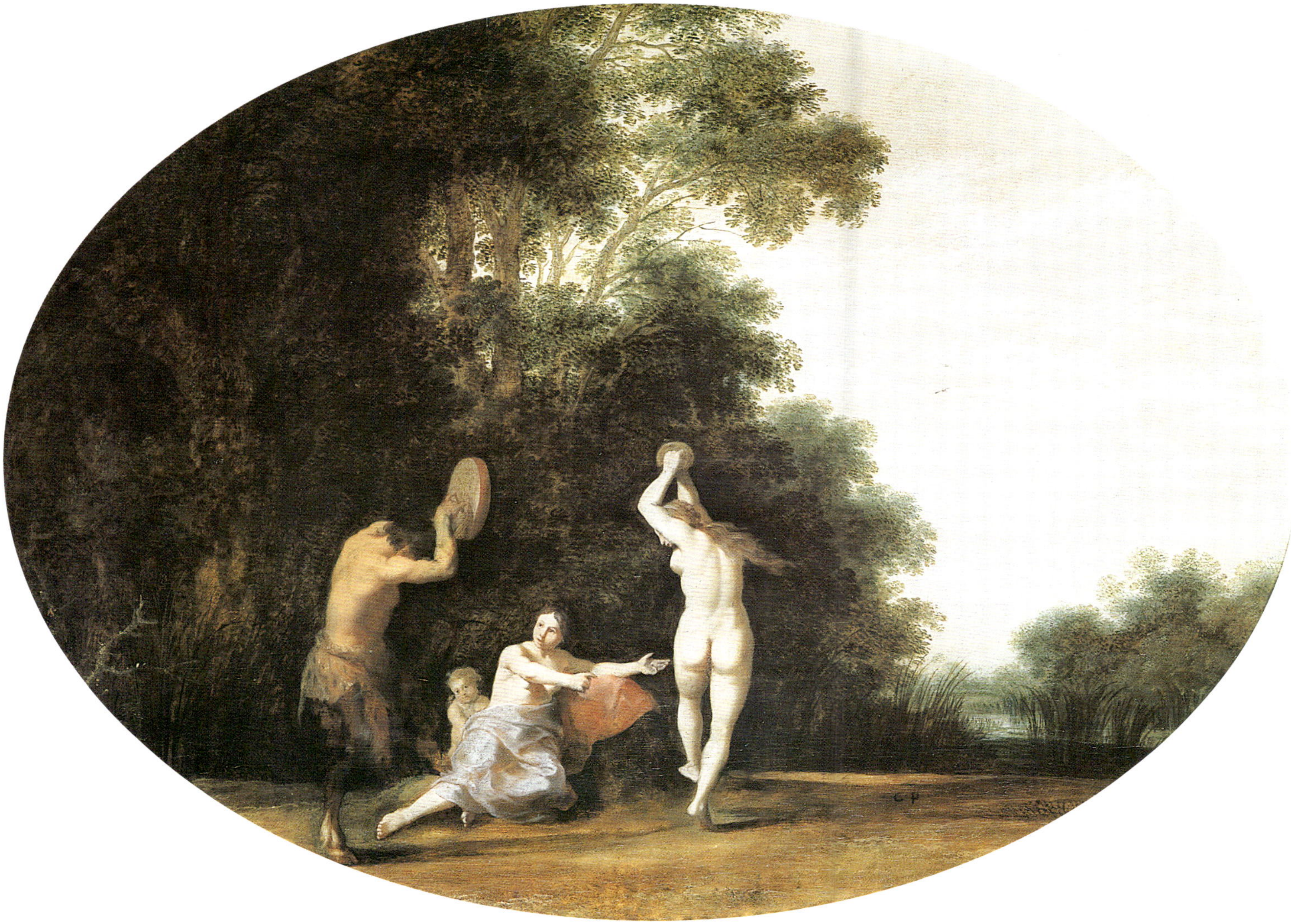

echoed these speculations, I chose this small painting by an obscure seventeenth-century Dutch artist, except that it is one of the works I return to every time I visit Dulwich and its almost awkward figures spoke to me even as a schoolboy.

This strange little image which seems, despite its tambourines, so silent, has its own modest but archaic truth. It is the least flamboyant version possible of the Arcadian myth. I find myself believing in this simultaneously chaste and sexy group of satyr and nymph and bacchic lady and imagine that Poelenbergh, an ordinary sort of chap, had, while out walking, come across them doing what we see them doing here and had painted them when he got home.

In a sense it is the nearest thing to cave art in the collection. For all its well-mannered style, dance and trance and the Great God Pan are not far off.

[1] *'Africa: the art of a continent'* was shown at the Royal Academy of Arts, London in 1995 and subsequently in Berlin (Gropiusbau) and New York (Guggenheim Museum). The catalogue is published by Prestel.

[2] These do not always take expected forms. Among the Tutsi of Rwanda the basket is the focus of artistic expression and, most basically, in one African tribe of cattle farmers it is the beauty of their beasts' markings that is most admired. Those cattle with the finest patternings are highly prized and give status to the owner and the best can be exchanged for many animals with less beautiful markings.

R is for Reality

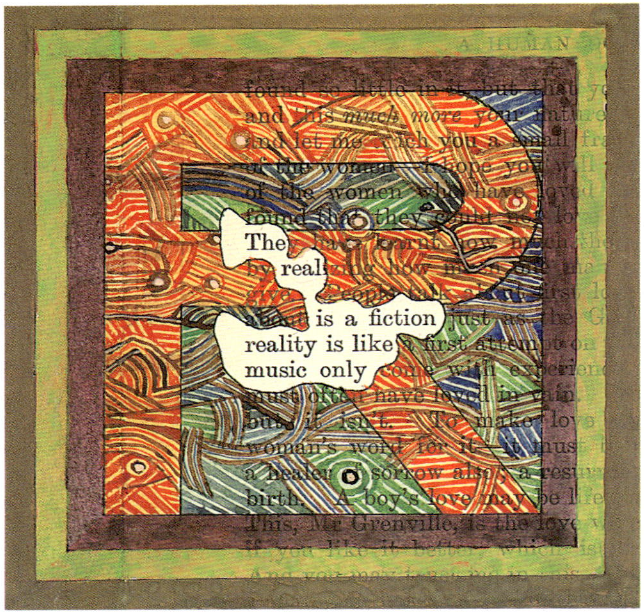

Reality is a trick of the light. Imagine painting from a female life-model in the late afternoon. As the gloom gathers you strain to see what you have been painting: finally when it is too dark you switch on the light. Suddenly nothing on your canvas seems to relate to what you see. With a new light source, different both in nature and direction, no shading or shadow, no colour or highlight is now true, yet the model's reality has not changed in any way: she is the same person in the same pose and very recognisably herself. Nature's essence must dwell elsewhere than in any particular accident of light.

The same is true of the line drawing. However realistic someone might call your drawing, no one can point to this black boundary on the model herself. She carries neither shading nor a wiry outline around with her. These are conventions of notation on the part of the artist and his audience who (from the time of the outlines of animals drawn in caves) have had thirty-thousand years to learn the language.

All the pictures reproduced in this book could be described in terms such as 'realistic', 'life-like', or 'naturalistic', but reality itself cannot be simultaneously in the style of van Dyck (p.41), Canaletto (p.16) or Poussin (p.25, p.63). These painters deal with what they say in a code as artificial as the rhetoric of formal speech.

Since painting in any case leaves out most of what we experience (its taverns do not smell, its seas will not drown us, its battles make no noise), it can be said to make no attempt to convince us that anything is really there. When art does divert to illusion it becomes a kind of temporary trick that relies on our cooperation.[1]

Art's purpose is to give us a world to see the world by. In doing so it tells some kind of truth but, by its very variety of styles and manners of presentation, confirms that truth is not one thing seen one way.

The Linley sisters come to haunt us from the eighteenth century. They speak of a life that was only *then*, as well as one that is for ever. They become (like the novels of Jane Austen) a touchstone of their time, so that costume drama can plunder them and feminist historians can use them as examples of women's circumscribed role in the period. Such things can be taken from the picture and leave it undiminished, whereas a lesser painting can, like a fashion plate, be used up and discarded since its apparent reality consisted only of information.

Gainsborough's theatre is coherent (as Lely's does not quite manage to be, p.39). The fury of his notation is surprising. Up close the costumes are a chaos of streaks and blobs and the land-scape is hand-written in an abstracted personal shorthand.[2] His technique was to use very long brushes so that he could paint on the canvas from an appropriate viewing distance and could stop when it 'worked'. The sisters are real in their own terms but do not disturb *our* reality which remains unchallenged. The Linleys were a dynasty of musicians and Gainsborough's love of music and women and his friendship with the family are present in the portrait. It is music alone that is realistic among the arts because it represents itself.

---

[1] For which we use the French term, *Trompe-l'oeil* (literally 'trick the eye'), since it is designed to deceive.

[2] Gainsborough is frequently reported to have brought little clumps of grass and twigs into the studio from which he concocted his background landscapes.

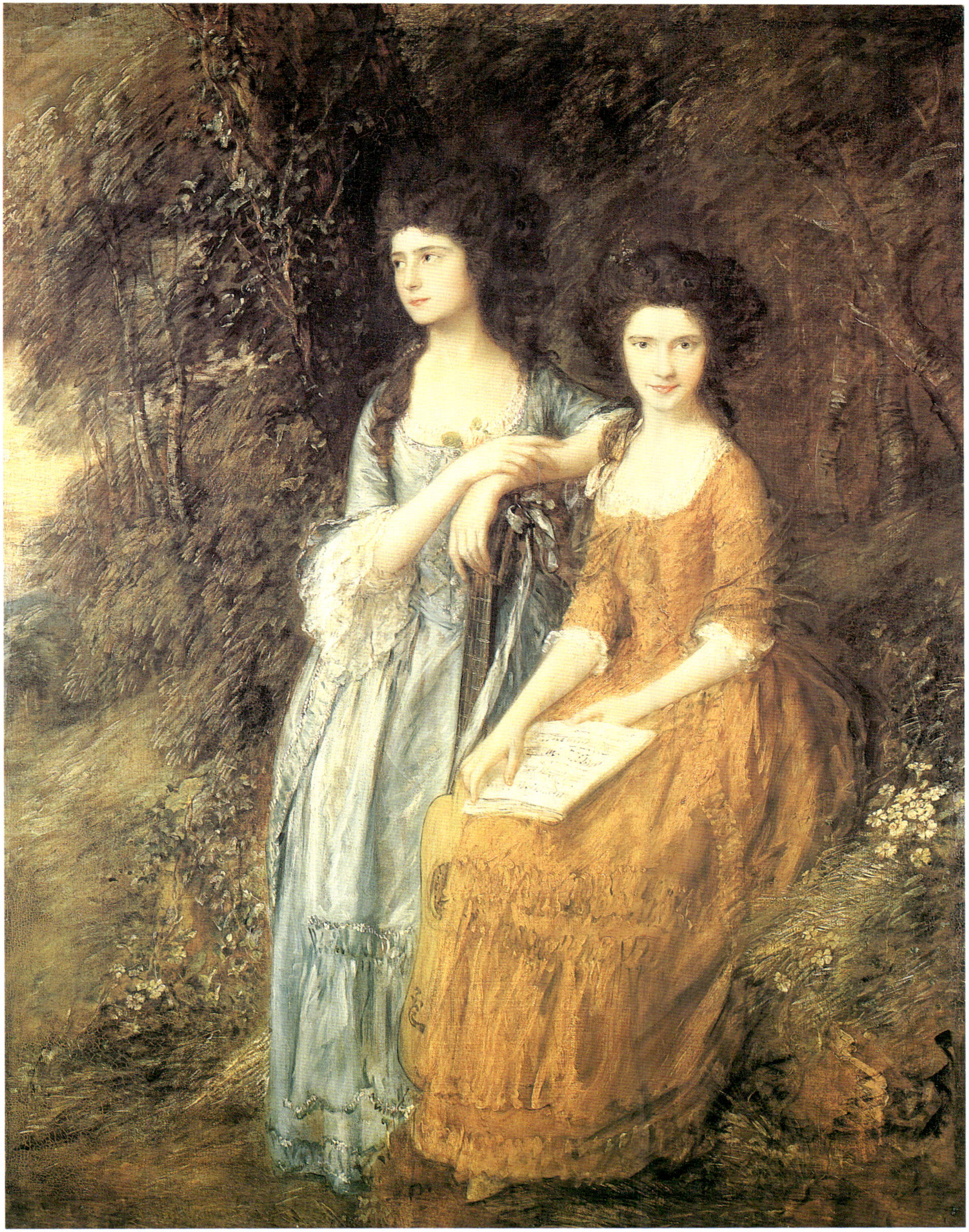

S is for Still-life

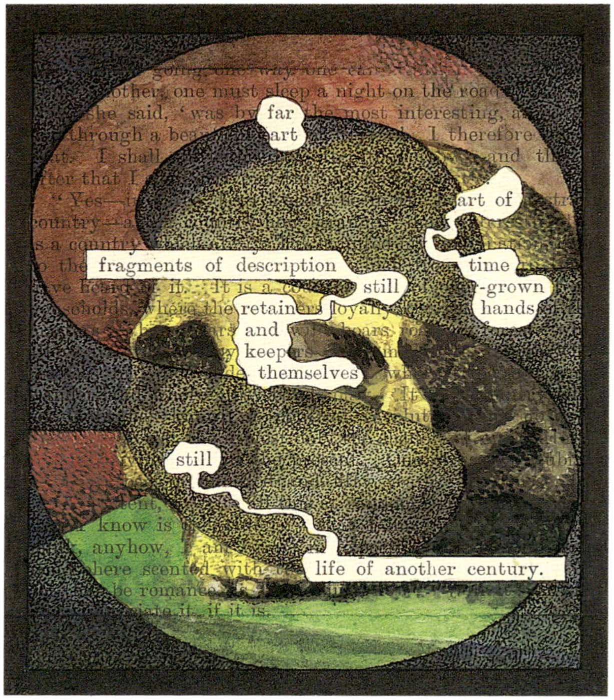

Still life occurs in the backgrounds of pictures before it comes into its own as an autonomous subject. Some of its greatest exponents never painted a still-life as such.[1]

The most frequently depicted item in this context from the beginning of still-life to the present day is the skull.[2] The one quoted in the initial letter comes from the standard seventeenth-century portrait of an unknown man (also reproduced on this page) where it teams up with another staple of the genre, the book.
A skull, as Hamlet found, is an eloquent thing. Its usual function in painting (as in Shakespeare's play) is to remind one of the inevitability of death and the consequent vanity of human wishes: a picture in this mode was referred to by the Latin word *vanitas*.

The image opposite, from a century or so earlier, is by an unknown artist. It is a wonderful example of how a quite awkwardly painted work can be both intense and carry complete conviction. It compels one not to pass it by as one might many more seemingly brilliant canvases from more gifted hands. Without possessing any of the facility of van Dyck or the graceful ease of a Gainsborough the artist has laboured nonetheless to produce an unforgettable ikon.

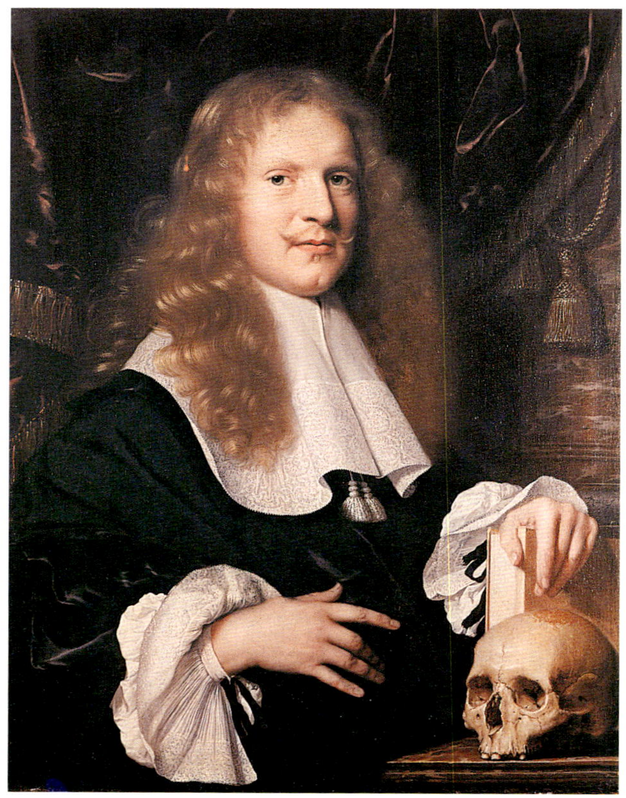

Both in French (*nature morte*) and in Italian (*natura morta*) still-life becomes 'dead nature'. Perhaps these translations reflect its frequent association with death more frankly than the discreet English term: yet they seem to deny it an occasional innocent pleasure in the world of objects. To the artist who customarily worked with its opposite, the live model, still-life could be a useful alternative. One does not have to pay an apple to sit still; moreover it will never fail to turn up and will not require cups of coffee every hour. Anything gazed at with the scrutiny required for painting will acquire some resonance and it is almost impossible to paint one object in conjunction with another without some meaning attaching itself to the result: symbolic opportunities abound.

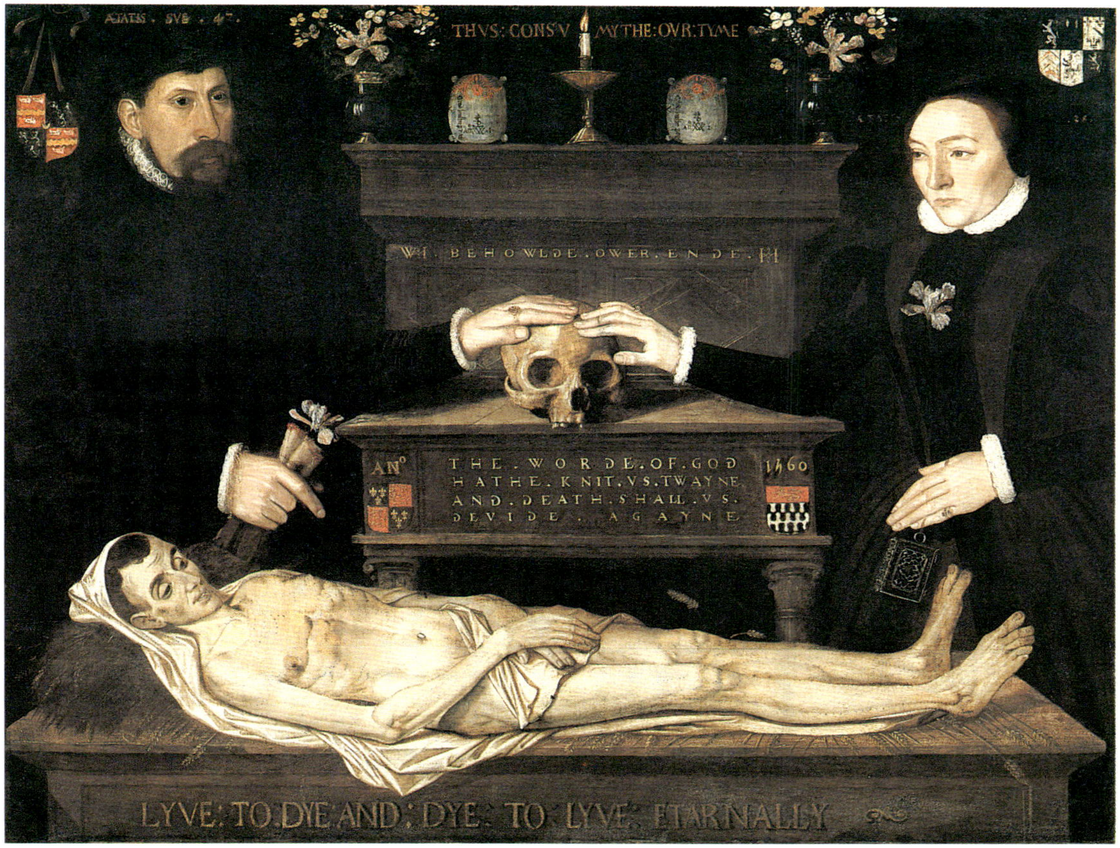

It contains still-life elements in grim abundance every one of which points insistently at our impermanence; the candle that must soon burn to its end, he flowers that will fade and, of course, the inevitable skull. Various writings appear, disguised as inscriptions on furniture etc, and all variations on the theme of mortality. The corpse is the ultimate gesture in this vein and less impersonal than the skull (which could always be a studio prop) and is, literally, life stilled.

At the time of their marriage the pious couple almost twenty years apart in age, acknowledging that death will divide them, embrace the christian certainty that it will finally unite them again. Initially the picture seems morbid in the extreme but as devout christians their belief is ultimately joyful. Meanwhile art unites them as one of the inscriptions spells out:

> When we are dead and in our graves
> and all our bones are rotten
> By this shall we remembered be
> When we should be forgotten

While not questioning the sincerity of Mr and Mrs Judd, it seems an odd hedging of bets. This is more transparent in Pieter Nason's portrait of the unknown man. He seems to say 'Immortalise me in my humble transience', as if we could not work out that humility, the assertion of personal transience and the desire for well-dressed immortality are suspect bedfellows. Ironically, the Judd situation in his case has been reversed and, unlike his painter, it is he who has been forgotten.

---

[1] A jug on a shelf in a Velasquez or some domestic objects in a Vermeer can have a vibrant life while taking an unassuming role in the composition.

[2] The greatest of twentieth-century painters of the still-life (perhaps the greatest ever) was Picasso. The skull makes a frequent appearance, especially in the bleak studies he painted during the Second World War.

T is for Theatre

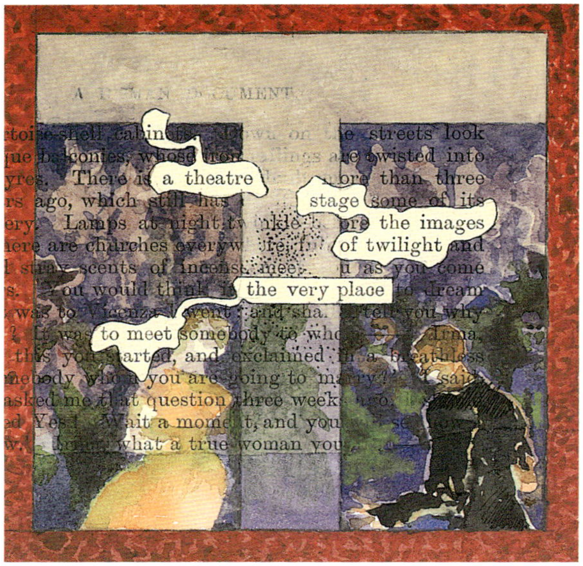

In a traditional theatre the proscenium arch marks the boundary between your reality and that of the actors on the stage. You always know that you are in the audience and not the play: at least your body knows all for, although at the beginning of the drama the actors and audience are completely separate, it doesn't take long (if the play is good and the cast is compelling) for your mind to migrate to the stage and inhabit its world.

The process of entering the space and atmosphere of a painting [1] (where trees, cows and flowers can sometimes take the place of actors) has its similarities. Because, in contrast to the theatre, you have not paid to see a particular single work in a gallery the business of engaging with a painting is more voluntary. Yet a picture that you passed by yesterday might, today, suddenly stop you in your tracks: you accept its invitation and look at it with new interest and even yield to it.

If what it depicts is some narrative captured in a frozen moment you may see the theatre echoed in the gestures of its painted people. The characters in paintings signal their grief, joy, frenzy and love in movements whose code is taken from the stage. Some of these stylised expressions and gesticulations may, with the changing taste of theatrical production, seem over-rhetorical but many will still be familiar.

Poussin, (as one might almost guess from his paintings) in those winter evenings when light was insufficient for painting, was in the habit of assembling tiny theatres peopled by clay models which he would arrange and rearrange as trial groupings for his compositions (p.25, p.63). These he would illuminate with strategic candles and draw the shadowy result.

No pictures occupy a universe so full of theatrical reverie as those of Watteau from whose fêtes and revels one can never imagine anyone doing anything as prosaic as going home. His actors and actresses live only in their silks and satins and cannot leave the dream.

Here it is the interval of a ball. The band has struck up once more while professional dancers occupy the floor to entertain the courtly guests. It is hard to say in this haunted assembly where real life begins and ends: they all have a role rather than an existence. Even the arch of what seems to be a stage points away from us into a park that might well be a theatre backdrop. The smallness of scale and the fragility of the little figures in their rigid costumes have all the ethereal enchantment of Prospero's famous speech.[2] At a touch they will vanish. Nevertheless these people did have a material existence and sat in a real studio for Watteau to draw them. His work singles him out as uniquely theatrical among artists, as if his short life was led in a band of strolling players who sought out such architectural never-never lands as this, surrounded by improbable parks, settled upon them like butterflies and resumed their delicate and insubstantial mummery.

[1] The short cut to this experience can be made via a cardboard tube (p.20), which like the theatre renders everything dark except for the image.

[2] Our revels now are ended. These our actors as I foretold you, were all spirits and are melted into air, into thin air …
(*The Tempest* Act IV, Sc. 1).

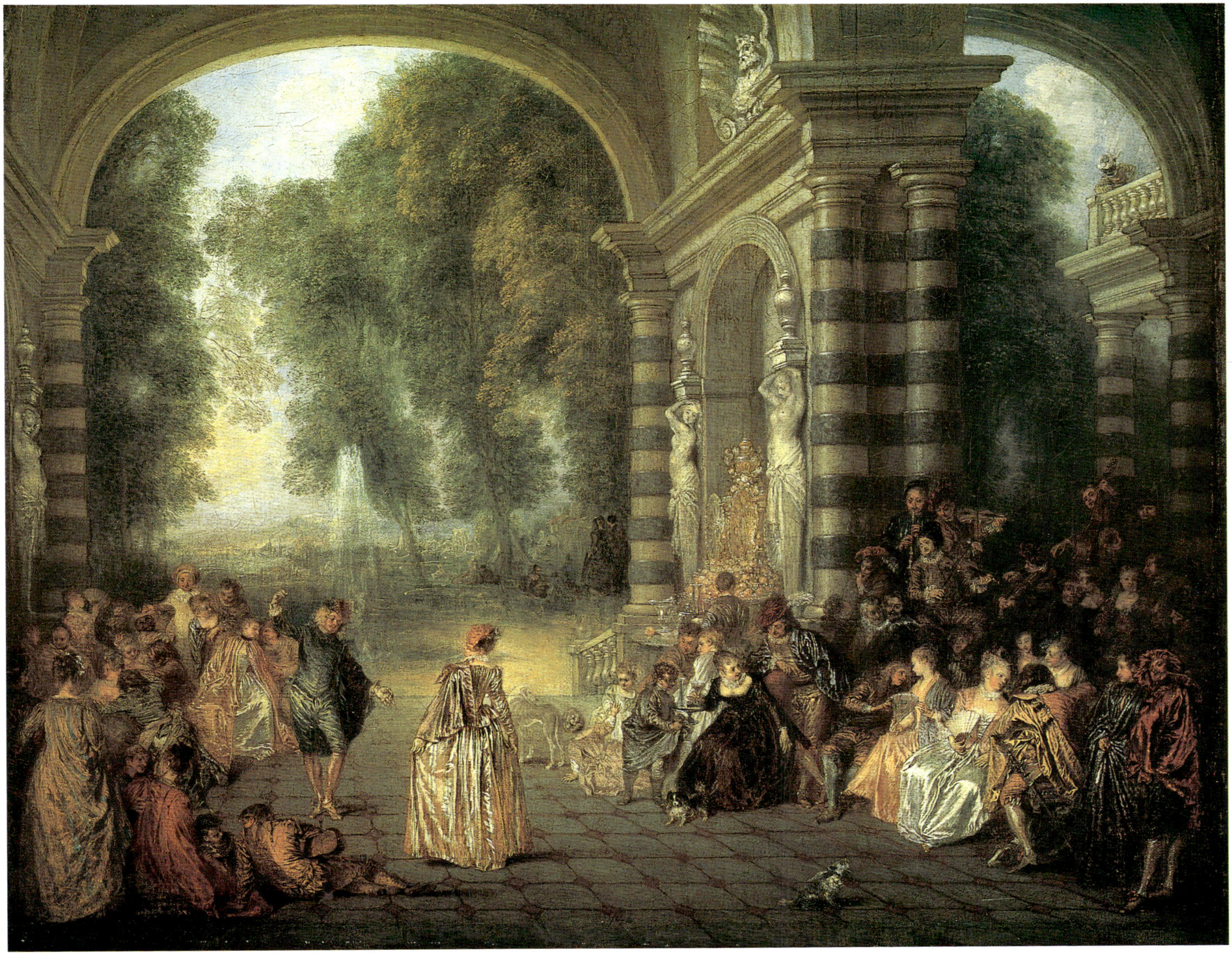

U is for the Unconscious

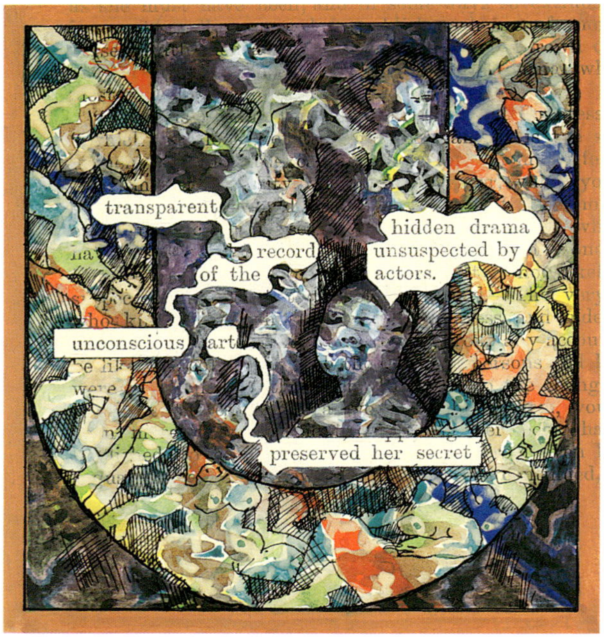

The strange energy that makes great art comes from sunken wells long covered over. Artists are often surprised with what they dredge up.

All the paintings in the Dulwich Picture Gallery were made before Freud identified and defined the unconscious and Jung poeticised its workings. It is perhaps a bit unfair to put old masters on the psychiatrist's couch or to say that an artist working before the word 'psychology' even existed [1] was depicting loneliness or indulging his erotic fantasies (or both) when he himself thought he was painting a vase of flowers.

However, to examine pictures in this way shows the advantage shared by artists when the Jekyll of the conscious mind was innocent of the Hyde of the unconscious. The tension between hidden fears and stifled anxieties, and the attempt to represent the world coherently might be one of the richest sources of creative energy.[2]

Thus there is a large paradox at work. The underlying message of psychoanalytic thought is that knowledge of something (dark urges or secreted memory) releases you from its grip. What you bring out into the open loses its sinister power over you and does not, as in its suppressed state, leak out only in disturbing dreams and damaging neuroses. In art, it almost works the other way round: the unconscious images that rise unrecognised and uninvited to inhabit the work give it its unique and particular character. They are bottles from our best and lowest cellar, provisions from our deepest store.

Our sexual drives and their coded picturing are now known to us: they can only be used consciously and by choice. No longer can the imagination dwell naively in the pubic undergrowth among phallic rocks and vulvate caves. The train now enters the tunnel with a knowing wink: the cheapened orifice and devalued phallus have become the stock-in-trade of advertising.

Here from the pre-Freudian past the solid Sir Joshua (founder and first president of the Royal Academy) in painting this allegorical portrait leaves so many traces of his healthily disturbed psyche that it needs no expert to make from it an inventory of sensual forms.[3] The lower half alone is a wonderful abstraction, a velvet orgy of protuberance and fold. If the picture had been made in the twentieth century it would be thought dense with intended sexual symbolism.

[1] The weakness of Surrealism could be that it knows too well what it is up to. Expressionism has trouble also since, identifying anxiety (*angst*), it can add it to the surface excitement of the painting.

[2] Freud wrote a long essay on Leonardo da Vinci analysing his pictures in this way. One wonders what effect it would have had (other than making him smile) on Leonardo if he could have read it.

[3] Sir Joshua Reynolds. *Mrs Siddons as the Tragic Muse*, 1789. His zest for the painting is undiminished in this second version, a replica from his own hand (unusual at the time), commissioned for the high price of £735. Mrs Siddons was, as great actresses are today, an embodiment of female projection and male fantasy.

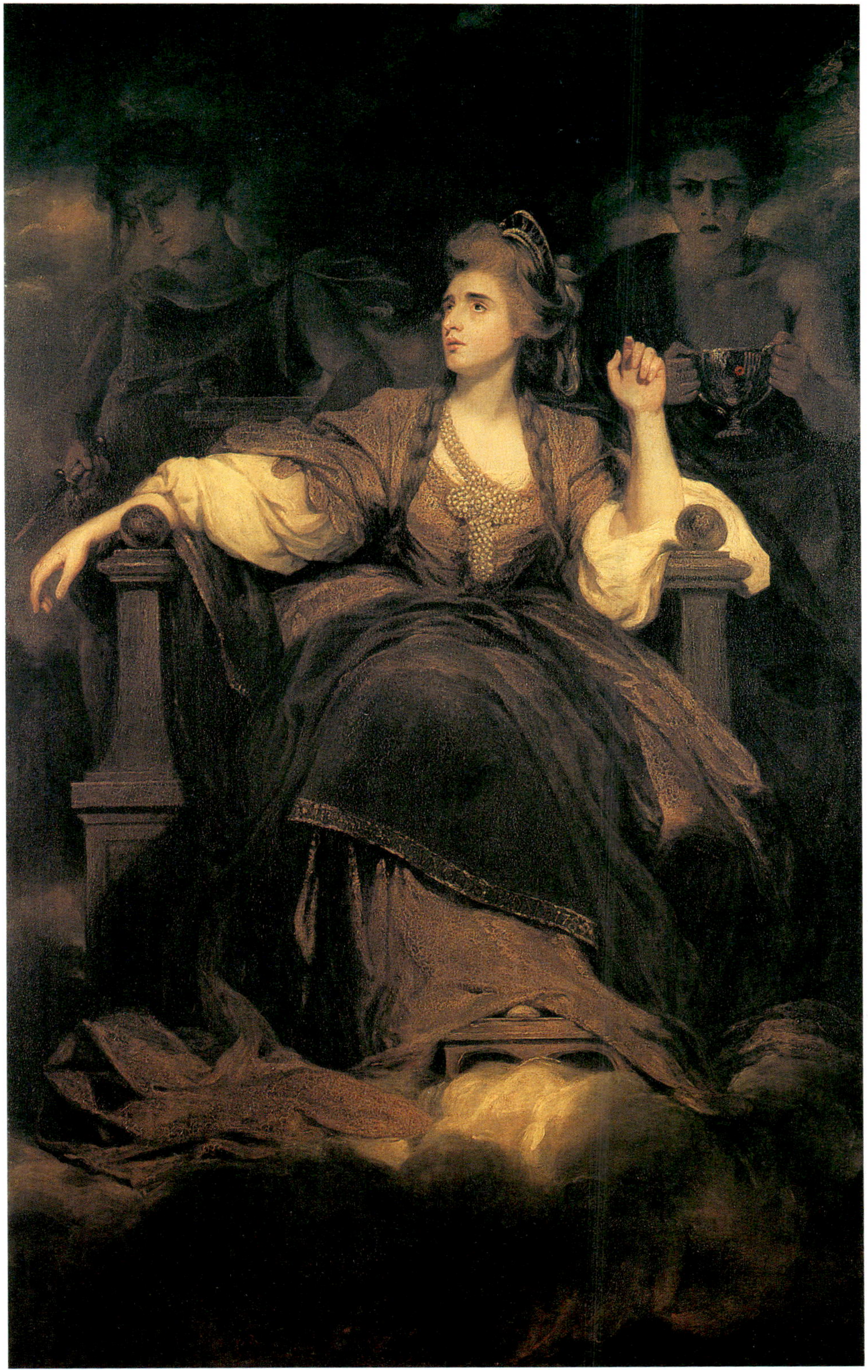

V is for Vision

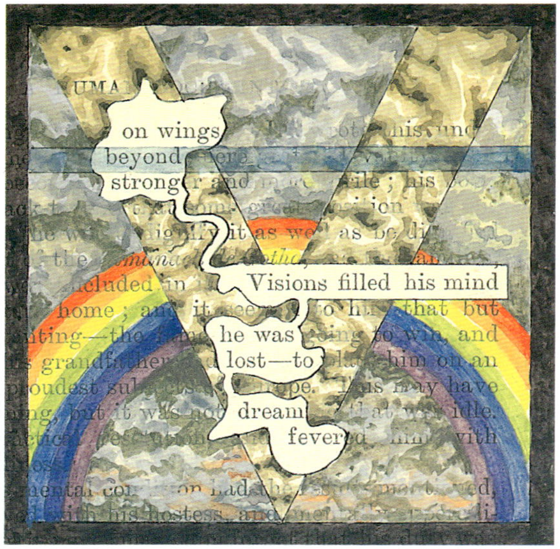

Vision is what we all have as a faculty, but visions are given to few. Good painters must have some heightened way of seeing (although in every-day life artists see the same things in the same way as everyone else). Painters, like poets and playwrights, dream on our behalf, just as the characters in classical and biblical mythology have their visions on behalf of the community, as here in *Jacob's Dream*.[1]

Realising a written vision is as hard as remembering dreams. In trying to pin them down we forfeit that elusive waywardness that is the stuff of our theatre of the night. Here on a tiny stage this little painting simultaneously shows us the tangible earth and a believable dreamer as well as the angelic denizens of the opening heavens, all linked by a thread of light.

This artist's dream therefore is the dream of a dreamer dreaming together with a dream of his dream. It seems probable that he painted it late in life. An artist is one who holds on to that world of childhood, vision and fantasy which usually gets lost as people grow into adults. Most tiny children seem able to make imaginative, excited images. By adolescence these have usually turned into stiff representations of a prosaic world: thereafter they vanish entirely. The adult, who says he or she can't draw anything, once painted vibrant visions of monsters and landscapes or free and uninhibited abstracts in colours which defied convention. Only the artist keeps the pot of dreams boiling all his life.

Another kind of phantasm involved in this small masterpiece is the dream that people weave around a name. For centuries when it was attributed to Rembrandt this picture was thought particularly beautiful. It was talked about as 'a perfect miracle' and 'wondrous'. When this dream of attribution was finally shattered in 1946, by the discovery of the little-known Aert de Gelder's signature, it retreated into obscurity as a charming work by a minor artist,[2] more likely now to be described as 'very nice'. I think its first admirers were right, even if they had to be bribed with a name.

[1] Jacob's Dream in the Jewish mythology of the Book of Genesis is of a ladder reaching to heaven on which he beheld the angels descending and ascending. The painter, here, convincingly makes his ladder from those beams of light we see striking the earth when the sun shines from among the clouds.

[2] Aert de Gelder, after a junior apprenticeship, went on at the age of sixteen to study with the ageing and by then neglected Rembrandt. This picture may have been painted half a century after Rembrandt's death. Although Rembrandt himself made beautiful versions of this same dream subject, he never achieved the innocent poetry of this work.

W is for Winter/Weather

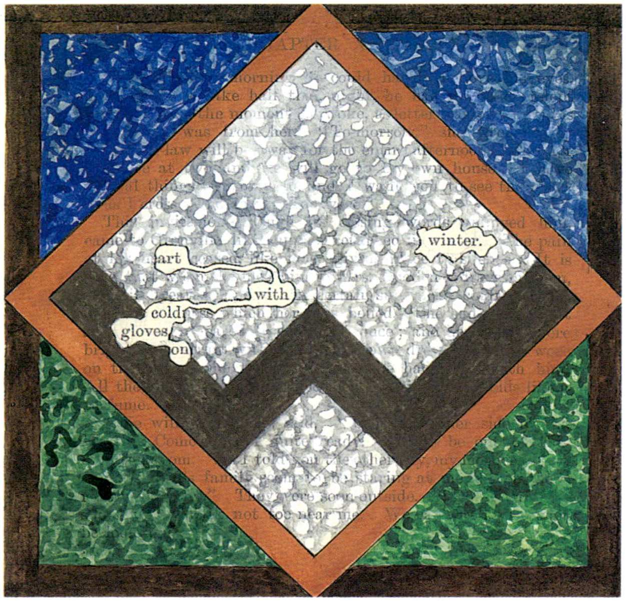

Weather is a great transformer of things, requiring them to be looked at and described anew. In Northern countries, the poetics of weather becomes a subject in its own right. The seasons parade themselves in all western art but winter was the special stock-in-trade of artists from what used to be called the Low Countries. It was the particular speciality of two interlinked dynasties of painters, the Teniers and Bruegel families.[1]

In a flat world of so much water with reliable snows and freezings-over a winter culture developed with its own occupations and pastimes all of which were eventually swallowed up in the idea of the Picturesque (p.34).

What is certain about winter views is that they dispel any idea of art representing what the artist saw as if he was painting his picture on the spot. To stand still at a blown-about easel, brush in frozen hand to paint this wintriest of winter scenes would not be the act of a sane man, however dedicated. Once again we see that painting is largely a cooked and not a raw activity.

At the same time as making this work from notes and sketches Teniers probably had other pictures in progress on other easels of more summery prospects. The information would be stored to eke out the dark days and many a cold studio boasted a picture on the go of burgeoning trees against blue skies.[2]

Such good husbandry is part of the metaphor of this composition, a country landscape that provides an inventory of winter sports and activity with a special focus on an important ritual: the killing of a pig, an act of the first big freeze of the waning year. The pig will serve the family for provisions until Easter is on the horizon and no part of it will be wasted.

Neither conventional grammar nor geometrical devices are brought in to assist this original and atmospheric canvas. The work of winter is to isolate things and make people dark and small, either solitary or huddled in unheroic groups. The human creature that struts through benign sunlit landscapes is cut down to size in the bitter season, for which nature has not fitted him with fur or feather. The wind blows the clouds and makes the few remaining leaves shudder on the trees; all is dispersed, and even the image itself does not shelter from the frozen day.

This is a picture that triumphs by being absolutely at one with its subject. Even the nearby roofs seem to collude by spelling the appropriate initial 'W'.

---

[1] The relationships of the Teniers dynasty are themselves a mystery, as well as their output. However hard they had worked, they could not have made all the thousands of pictures that bear their name.
David Teniers the younger (son of David Teniers the elder) married the daughter of Jan Bruegel the elder in 1637. This statement alone might persuade anyone to leave such matters to the experts.

[2] One of Teniers' jobs was to copy the (mostly Italian) pictures in the collection of his master, the governor of the Spanish Netherlands.

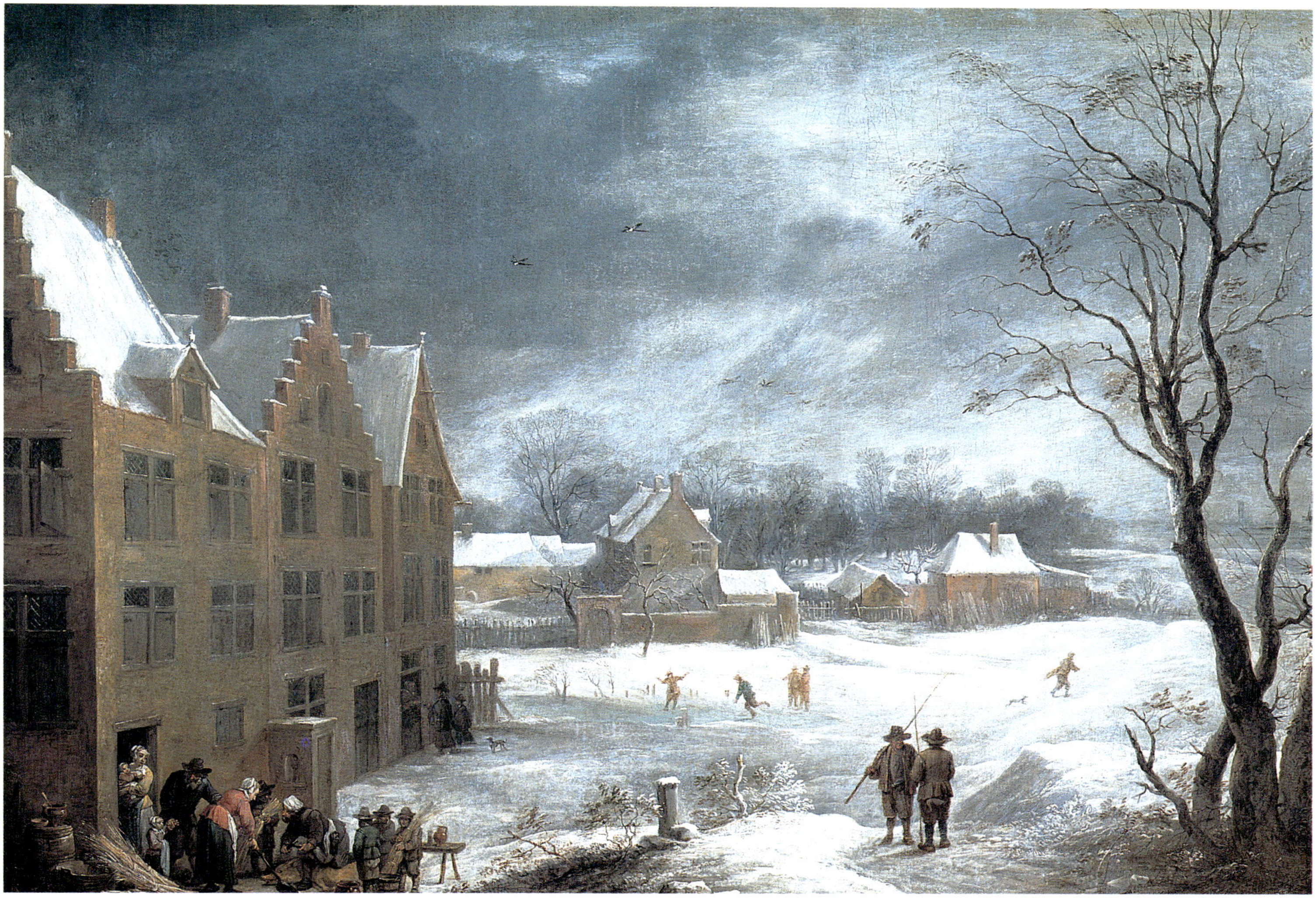

X is for 'x' (or who, what or where?)

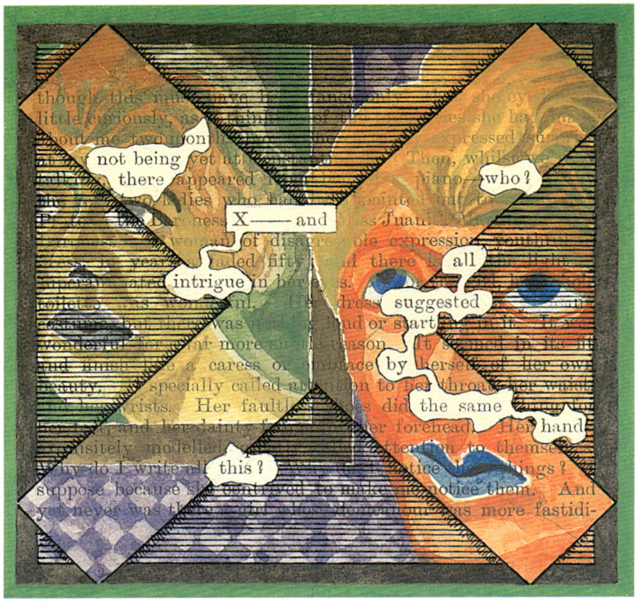

We get little opportunity to make our own judgements in art museums. We are invariably tempted to sneak a look at labels which condition our responses. Surveys carried out in art galleries recently, seem to suggest that people on average spend only a couple of seconds looking at each picture, over half of which is taken up with reading the label. Now that the labels themselves, in many institutions, tend to carry more and more information (biographical details of the painter, points of interest in the picture, etc.) the traffic must be getting slower: congestion begins to be the rule in popular exhibitions and a kind of 'gallery rage' cannot be far away.

The labels to both these portraits however detain no visitor since they both read simply *'Artist unknown: portrait of an unknown man'*, leaving us completely free to make up our own minds whether to give them the time of day and liberating us to the unnerving situation of evaluating them for ourselves.

The bearded head certainly looks Italian, probably from the artistically vague territory of Central Italy. It used to carry the optimistic designation 'Annibale Carracci'[1] but the Carracci family are a well-known dustbin into which all unidentified Italianate pictures used to be put.

The other picture is certainly North European, somewhere on that axis from Switzerland, through Germany and the Low Countries, and ending with continental artists working in England. The early attribution to Holbein is also optimistic (though the Holbein family included, as well as the great Hans, many journeyman artists) yet a stylistic area is indicated. Beyond this, art history hardly dares to tread.

But what of their quality? The Italian head seems to me a slippery job, all style and no substance. It is the generic head of any forgettable saint in any altarpiece in an area of ten thousand square miles. It may be painted from life or from a drawing but its origin must surely be one of those itinerant models, who, being the bearers of strong heads and well cultivated beards, went from studio to studio posing for pictures of Saint Peter, Saint Paul, Saint Jerome or any other elder of the church. He is the identikit saint that you will see in a thousand altarpieces, here painted with vivacity by a minor artist.

The other is a completely different case. Here is a man straining to be known painted by an artist yearning to be remembered. What the painting lacks in poetry it makes up for in directness and honesty. This burgher with his peasant features yet clear and intelligent gaze has no visual attributes other than a book of an unequivocally devotional appearance: it announces a piety we might well have guessed from the face. The hands seem to belong to him and their slight puffiness is consonant with the head and body. Hands in portraits often give nothing away since it was quite normal to use a studio assistant to model them (and another to

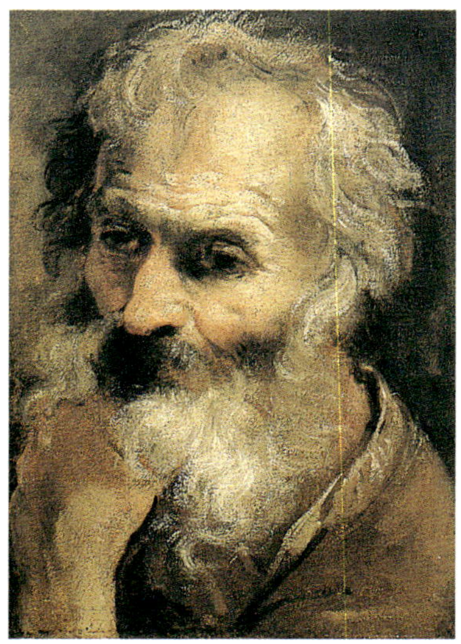

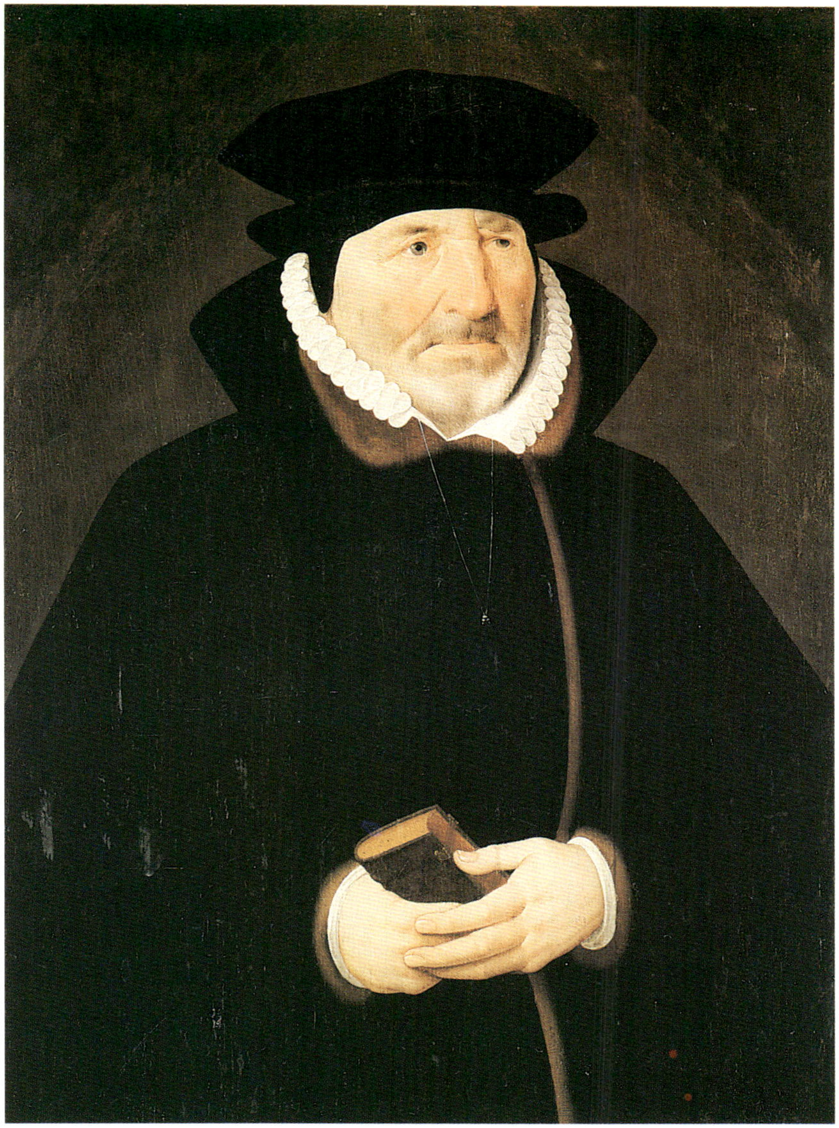

paint them) until well into the nineteenth century. Here they seem to belong to the sitter and to be painted by the painter. The cap and ruff might suggest to a fashion historian (one of that useful breed who can sometimes date a picture to within a few months via the ancient equivalents of hemline and type of trainer) some more precise location and period but I for one am happy to enjoy the picture in ignorance. The solidity and awkwardness of the image brings it into that family of provincial paintings (p.49) which give such anonymous pleasure in the galleries of the world. Whatever turns out to be the identity of painter and subject, if they are ever tracked down, we can say that it is a true portrait of a very particular individual executed with skill, insight and conscientiousness by an artist with none of the glib bravura of his distant Italian colleague. In case of fire one would certainly rescue first the old man with a book.

[1] The Carracci family were responsible for a huge output ranging from the brilliant to the workaday. Virtually every museum in the world has put the Carracci label on the work of one of their many imitators so that their own *oeuvre* has been diluted and a number of Central Italian masters are left anonymous.

Y is for Youth

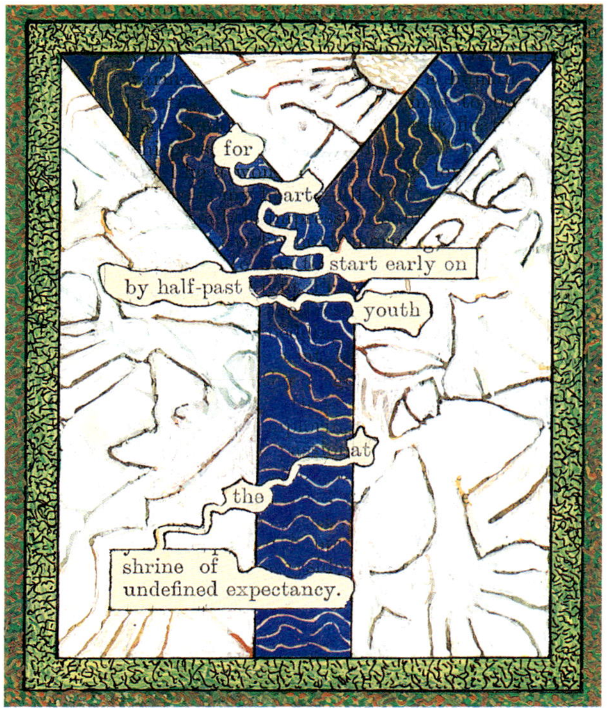

By the time present-day students are filling in forms to apply for places in art schools most of the painters of the past would have been established professionals. By the age of eighteen or so, Richard Wilson (p.35) had left Rome and was working as a portrait painter, Aert de Gelder (p.55) had finished both his apprenticeships, Peter Lely (p.39) was about to become a master of the Haarlem Guild, Gainsborough (p.47) had been working for some time as an engraver's assistant, and Canaletto (p.16) was a fully-trained scene painter in his father's workshop, etc. etc.

It may dismay today's young artists to think what a head start these painters had. Certainly their technical training was far in advance of anything on offer now, yet the compass of their education was often very narrow and a lack of general schooling fitted them for no other task. We forget the thousands upon thousands of artistic drudges that the apprentice system gave rise to. For every name that is represented in museums a huge forgotten band of assistants, drapery painters and studio skivvies, who alternated modelling with the grinding of colours and preparing of surfaces, died with their smocks on, unknown to posterity. An artist like Rubens would have a staff of almost twenty apprentices and helpers and his studio would also become the magnet for any brilliant young painter of the day.

One of these is the author of the only picture in the gallery painted by a teenager. Van Dyck entered Rubens studio as an independent master and would have been entrusted with important commissions. His art training had begun at the age of ten when he enrolled as a pupil of Hendrik van Balen. This opulent picture of Samson and Delilah is an amazing *tour de force* to have performed before the age of twenty. It seems almost like showing off in that it deals with all aspects of the business of narrative painting: complicated composition and grouping of figures, rendering of flesh and fabric, expression, depiction of youth and old age, handling of space and atmosphere, and mastery of colour. Even though it owes so much of its language and grammar to Rubens it is a true autonomous masterpiece.[1]

'Old Master' is an unfortunate term: I seem to remember thinking it referred as much to the age of the painter as his distance from me in time. Since then I've never quite lost the sense of surprise when figuring out from a museum label quite how young the great painters often were when they achieved their finest work.

Genius however is not solely related to early brilliance and many prodigies never fulfilled expectations.[2] The final pantheon of art includes many whose beginnings were clumsy or slow. Wonderful artists emerge, whatever system of apprenticeship or art schooling is current and the old masters of the future have taken and will take strange roads to arrive at their unpredictable destinations.

---

[1] The word masterpiece (and its French equivalent *chef-d'oeuvre*) originally meant a work done to establish professional qualifications and to gain entry into a guild.

[2] Of the painters who towards the end of the last century and the beginning of this were to change the whole face of western art only one (Picasso) was an early starter. Monet, van Gogh, Gauguin and Matisse all had tentative beginnings. Almost any facile contemporary would have shown more apparent promise than the young Cezanne.

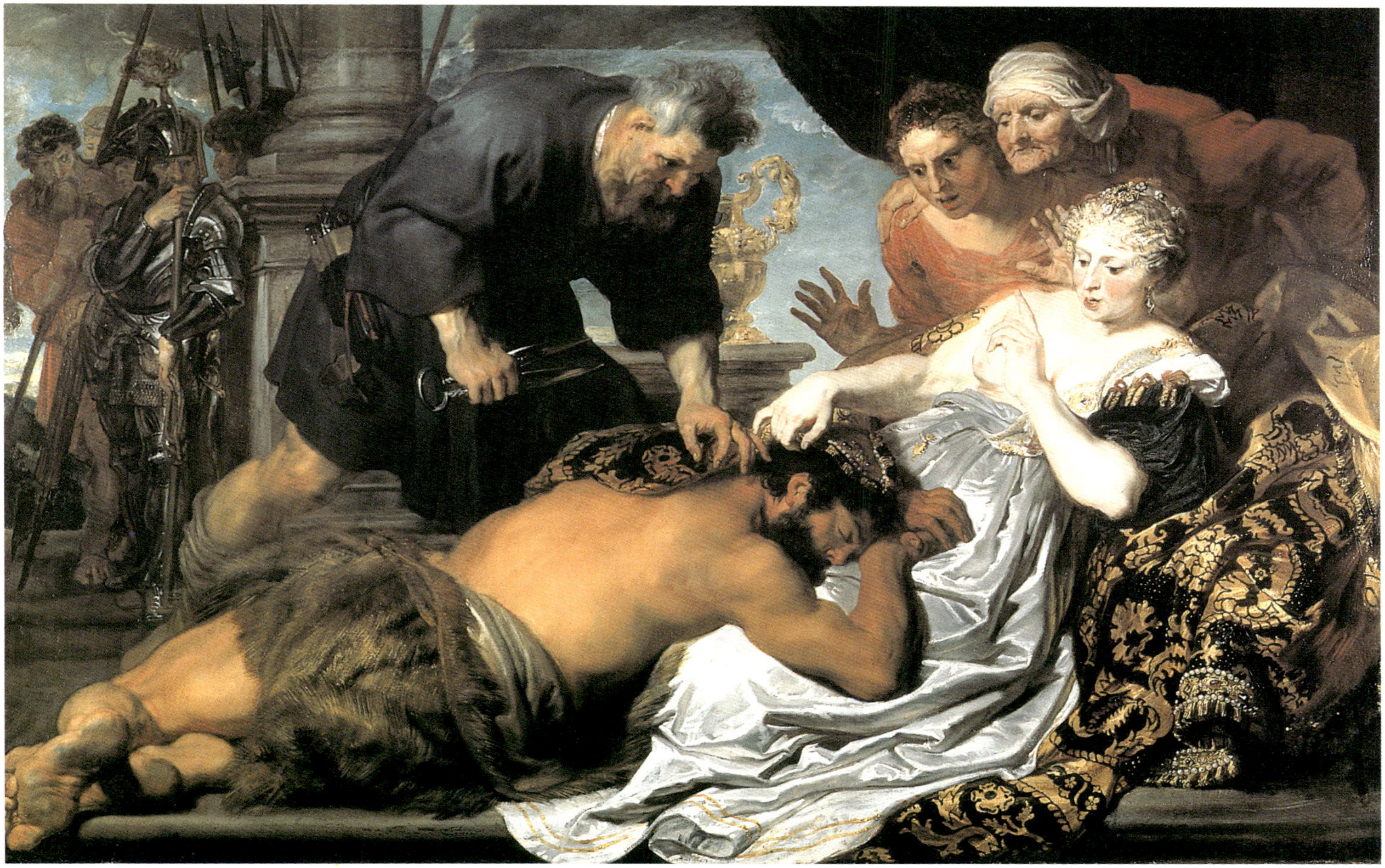

Z is for Zigzag

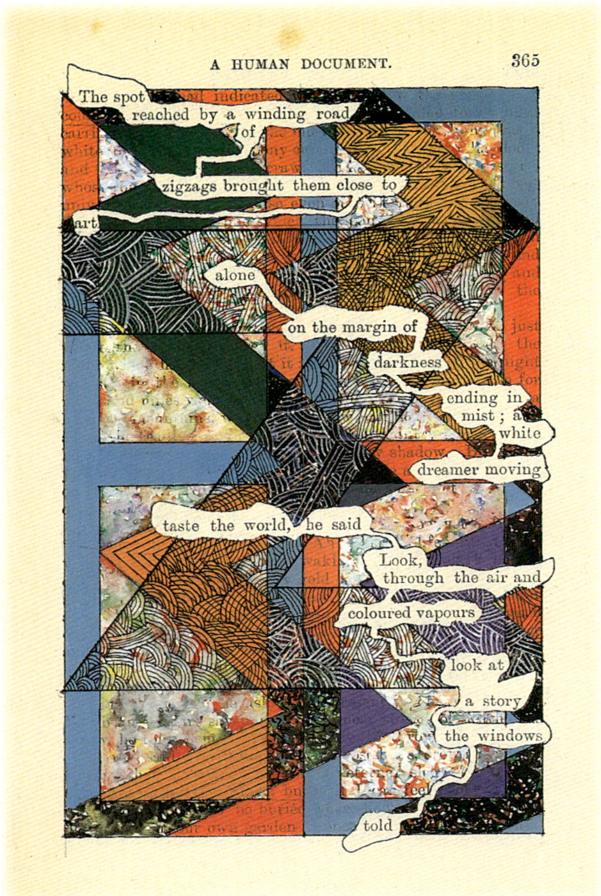

This book has itself zigzagged its way like a pinball in a machine through the Dulwich galleries and has bounced back and forth among the pictures. The alphabet served rather as a way of ensuring random collisions than as a mode of organising material. A similar path back through the letters would ring other bells and evoke other questions. No grand conclusion has ever been aimed at. The intention was always to direct the reader this way and that, hoping to increase appetite and curiosity and to seek questions rather than answers.

The analogy of the pinball machine matches the mechanics of so many paintings: the artist attempts to control the movement of your eye across the surface of his work so that you visit every part of the picture. To persuade your attention not to wander beyond the frame, he makes a series of zigzags so that, in imitation of the ball's trajectory, you keep on returning to the action.

Zigzaggiest of all is this drama by Poussin [1] in which the figures occupy the depth of the picture by seeming to be held inside a transparent egg. The surface of the painting however is violently criss-crossed with lines of direction, some obvious, some half-concealed yet all controlling the process of looking. Poussin's idea is to make you travel with his heroine from left to right.[2] She is the active figure and the arrows of direction are metaphors of her haste. She sweeps on in her pointed mission to kill the sleeping enemy yet falls in love with him at the very moment she is about to stab him to death. This instant of timelessness within impulsive action is conveyed by the enfolding oval which the eye constantly revisits.

This, in the workings of a great operatic aria, is the kind of challenge that Verdi would relish, with the music surging forward to be caught and arrested in a sudden, vivid shift of mood.

All painters have had access to the grammar of such devices yet only the visionary can use the very language of composition to make this metaphor of love and death into an ever-still and ever-busy song of war and peace.

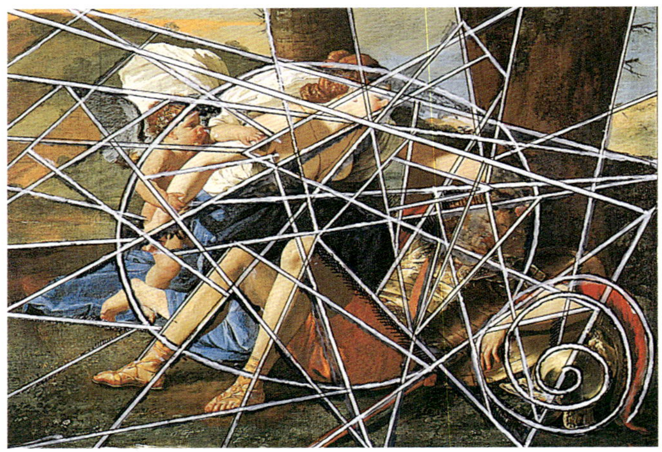

[1] The subject is taken from Torquato Tasso's *Gerusalemme Liberata* (1575) an Italian epic dealing with the liberation of Jerusalem by the first crusade. The poem never quite attained the mythical status of Homer, Virgil or Dante but was used as a frequent source by Poussin and others. Here Rinaldo, a christian hero, is under the dangerous enchantment of Armida, a Saracen enemy. Just as she is about to kill him, love (here represented by a restraining Cupid) overwhelms her.

[2] For the left to right orthodoxy see footnote 1, page 25. Here the artist exploits that trend, stilling the egg-shape by means of an emphatic spiral acting as a brake.

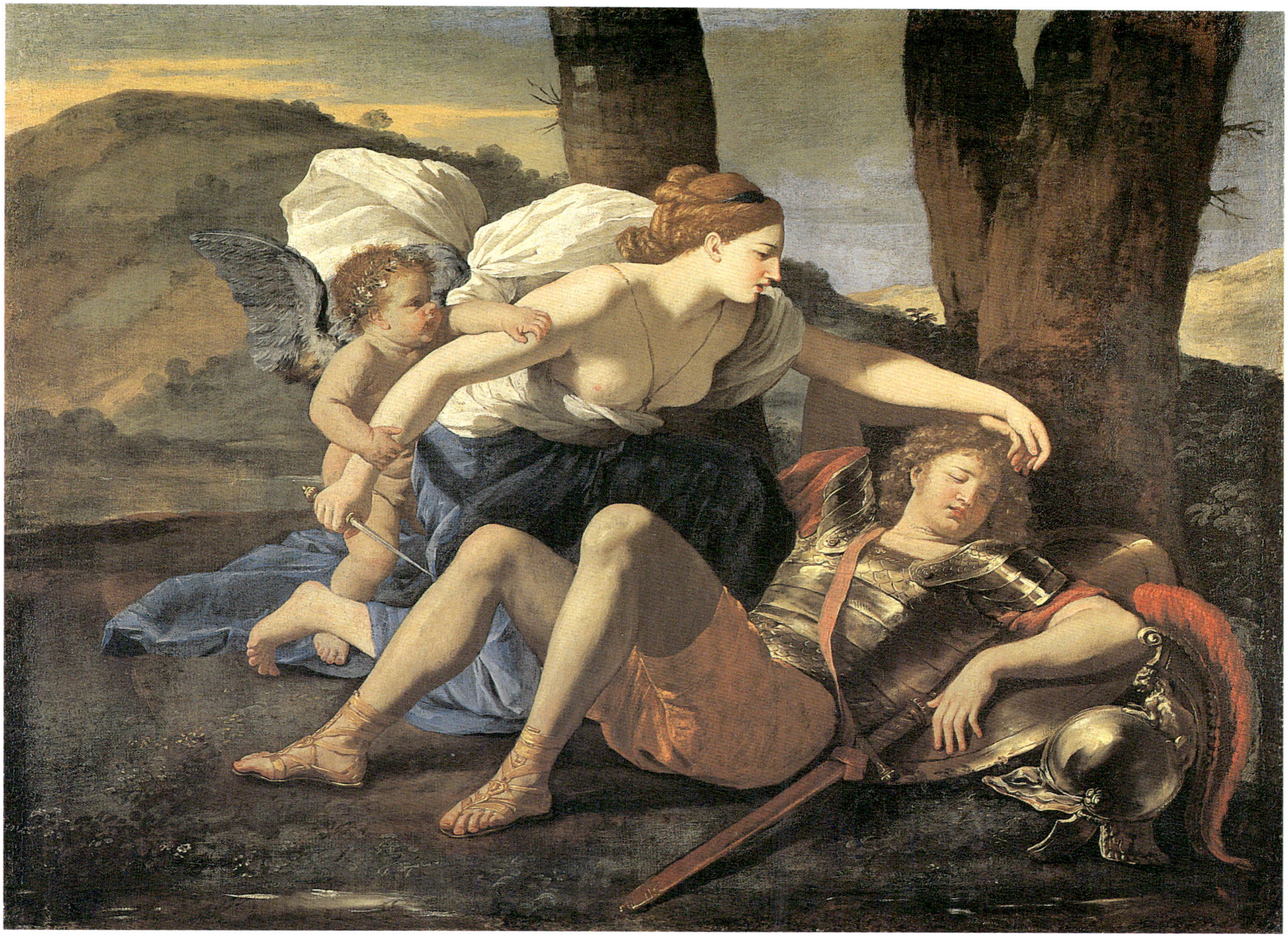

LIST OF PLATES

*All plates are oil on canvas except for those marked * which are oil on panel.*

This early Rembrandt appears as the frontispiece without an alibi except that there was a possibility of illustrating that of the three Dulwich Rembrandts I prefer. It was also Collam's favourite in the passage from Unhaunted Comma (1943) in which his famous definition of portraiture occurs. 'It's almost a surrogate self-portrait; a picture of a fellow citizen also young, ambitious and full of internal life. A portrait is one person in a room trying to be painted by another. Here the roles merge…'